D1366512

THE ULTIMATE MAN'S GUIDE™ TO

Losing Your Spouse and Keeping Your House

Surviving divorce with your health, sanity, sex life, spirit and finances intact

Howard Brian Edgar

PURPLE BUS PUBLISHING | WESTMINSTER

2005

Purple Bus Publishing
Westminster, CA 92683

The Ultimate Man's Guide™
is a trademark of H² Productions

Library of Congress Control Number Data

Edgar, Howard Brian, 1950 –
    The Ultimate Man's Guide™ to Losing Your Spouse and Keeping Your House: Surviving divorce with your health, sanity, sex life, spirit and finances intact / Howard Brian Edgar
    ISBN - 0-9741576-8-6

2004091685
CN

First Edition 2005

Cover, book and Ultimate Man's Guide™ mark designed by Gregory Trueblood

08 07 06 05   1 2 3 4 5 6 7 8 9 10

Manufactured in the United States of America

This publication contains the opinions and ideas of its author intended to provide helpful and informative material about the subject matter covered herein. The author and publisher assume no responsibility for errors or omissions and specifically disclaim any responsibility for any liability, loss or risk, personal or otherwise incurred as a consequence, directly or indirectly from the use and application of any of the contents of this book.

For all the men who want to navigate their divorce wars without getting killed.

HBE

Contents

Part Two: Surviving During Divorce

Part Three: Surviving After Divorce

Part Four: Where You'll Find More Help With Divorce

Introduction

"Experience is not what happens
to a man. It is what a man does
with what happens to him."

– Aldous Leonard Huxley, 1894-1963

Over 1.2 million couples divorce annually in the United States. That's 2.4 million adults and over one million children who experience the agonies of marital breakup firsthand. According to the latest U.S. Census Bureau reports, 58% of U.S. marriages now end in divorce, making America one of the divorce capitals of the world. Worse, the state of Oklahoma currently has a whopping 72% divorce rate. By contrast, the American divorce rate in 1900 was only 6%.

In addition to 60 of every 100 marriages ending by the 10th year, the overall divorce rate reaches over 70% nationwide by the 20th year. Which means there are tens of millions of adults and children coping with the aftermath of divorce. Today in America it is nearly impossible to meet anyone who has not experienced firsthand or been touched by divorce.

What makes this book different is that it's written for men from a male point of view based on 24 years worth of personal experience in the trenches of the marriage and divorce wars. And what you are about to read could save you a good deal of suffering and thousands of dollars on your divorce.

What Resources Do You Have?

American women have libraries, bookstores, TV shows, magazines and Internet sites filled with information and resources to help them cope with virtually every emotional, physical, spiritual and intellectual aspect of divorce. They also have over 800 university-based *women's studies* programs.

There are zero university-based men's studies programs. As for resources to help with divorce, men have a handful of books, a dozen or so websites and little else by comparison. The best of those resources are included in this book. And more.

It is sad that our society clings to a biased, erroneous belief that men don't need or want help with something as emotional as divorce. But divorce is far more than just emotions. The impact on your finances, future, health, self-respect and life can be enormous. Even if you can put aside the emotional impact, you cannot and should not ignore the rest.

What Have You Got to Lose?

One of the most pervasive myths of our time is that men gain economically from divorce while women suffer. This myth stems from a study conducted two decades ago by feminist Lenore Weitzman, author of the 1985 book *The Divorce Revolution*. At the time she wrote her book, Weitzman concluded that the average woman's standard of living after divorce dropped by 75% while the average man's rose over 40%. The media touted her research loudly. The resulting publicity and outcry – primarily from feminist groups – led to sharp increases in America's child support guidelines. Under the guise of "doing what's best for the children," feminists engineered a big financial win for women in divorce.

However, years later Weitzman admitted that her findings were vastly overstated *due to a huge mathematical error!* The entire premise of her book had been based on erroneous information and a major miscalculation.

Despite this, the myth that men gain economically from divorce is still entrenched in our society and is repeated even today by numerous writers and commentators. Among them are conservatives like Dennis Prager, feminists like Ann Crittenden and even outspoken "masculists" like nationally syndicated radio personality Tom Leykis, though Leykis has more recently realized that most men do not fare so well after all.

One of the nation's leading experts on the economics of divorce, Sanford Braver, PhD, is credited with exposing Lenore Weitzman's blunder. Braver believes that when all the facts are taken into account, including the tax advantages enjoyed by custodial parents, the vast majority of whom are women, the whole "men gain/women lose" idea is dead wrong. In fact, most statistics indicate that "men *lose*/women *gain*" is far more common and is, in fact, the pervasive phenomenon in American society.

The popular notion that men gain financially from divorce is absurd. The reality is that most men are ruined by divorce, and not just financially. That along with the current climate of male-bashing in American culture makes divorce a critical issue for men to confront. To survive, we have to face it head-on. We have to be proactive.

You Could Lose it All

It is not the intention of this book to demean women or insinuate that all women are evil. Nor is it the intention to say that all men should "lose the spouse and keep the house." In many cases, especially with children involved, men prefer giving up their homes to their ex-wives and children. It is often in the children's best interests to minimize the upheaval in their lives. If you don't want to keep your house for that reason, fine, as long as it's *your* choice.

But too many men who would choose otherwise still lose their homes and everything else they own, except their clothes, to divorce. Millions of American men have already lost their homes. Many have been forced to live in their cars or even cardboard boxes, suffering at the hands of angry, greedy, vindictive spouses, expensive attorneys, a greedy divorce industry and a faulty legal system. In fact, far too many men have lost everything, including their financial security, self-esteem, health, pride and zest for life after being brutalized by the American family court system and the feminist ideology it caters to.

Sadly, we also live in a society where people generally accept that it's okay for men to lose it all. After all, men become socialized to sacrifice their health for work, their bodies for sport and their lives for war. Why not our children, our homes, our finances and our well-being for divorce?

Sure there are violent bad men who have abused other men, their wives and children and deserve to lose their rights. But the vast majority of men are hard-working, devoted family men who are more likely to pay their bills, adore their wives and coach their kids' Little League teams in their spare time. Do they deserve to lose it all? Of course not. Yet, every day in America, men just like that are being completely devastated by divorce.

There are hundreds of thousands of men who have *never* recovered from divorce, even decades later. Devastated beyond repair, they've become shadows of their former selves. They avoid relationships and insulate themselves. They watch TV, go to the movies alone and play video games to pass the time. Lonely and reclusive, they often turn to alcohol and drugs to medicate their emotional pain away. They also commit suicide 4.5 times more often than women do. So who *really* comes out ahead in divorce? And how can you protect yourself against losing it all?

Twelve Strategies for Saving Your Assets

With so much to lose, the best time to plan for your divorce is long before you actually file the legal papers. The overriding concern, especially if you are still on the fence, is that you always think before you act. Don't do anything in the heat of a moment that you may regret later, and don't do anything illegal. If you are considering divorce, here are 12 strategies for protecting your assets before you or your spouse files.

1. Gather Intelligence on Her Income & Finances – Before you ever mention divorce to your spouse, nail down as much information about her income and financial status as possible. Is she salaried? Is she hourly? Is she self-employed? Does she own a business with or without partners? The best source for this information is your spouse. Be discreet when asking about her finances so you don't arouse her suspicion. Check her pay stubs or income tax documents such as W-2s for the most accurate information. Use stealth. The less you have to say to her or anyone else, the better.

2. Assess Your Family's Assets & Debts – Your assets include homes, cars, furnishings, jewelry, collectibles, savings, pensions, businesses and investments. Debts will include credit cards, bank loans, car loans, personal loans and mortgages. If your spouse manages the family finances, check her records. If you cannot access them and she won't give you any information, review your mail and see how much is being paid and to whom each month.

3. Stop Spending & Start Saving – Watch your spending habits to see where your money is going. Stop spending money on things you don't really need or cannot afford. Avoid making major purchases. Many men buy themselves expensive new cars when they are in the middle of divorce proceedings. Doing so will make you appear wealthier than you are and hurt your case if it goes to court. Bad move. Better move: Open a separate savings account in a different bank in your own name and start stashing some cash every week.

4. Divide Your Money Now! – Your request for a divorce may send her right to the bank, so take your half of the money in your bank accounts now. Put the money in a new account at a different bank or hide it until you are legally divorced.

5. Safeguard Property That Belongs to You – Remove anything of value from your home or residence that is indisputably yours. An angry woman will not think twice about taking or destroying your personal collection of CDs, DVDs or computer disks out of sheer spite. Remove your personal valuables and put them in storage or lock them away in a safe place.

6. Shore Up Your Credit – Send for a copy of your credit report and check it carefully for errors. Consider canceling credit cards or, at the very least, reducing the spending limits. Think ahead to your wife's reaction when you announce that you want a divorce. Women have been known to go on major spending sprees after hearing that kind of news. You don't want to be financially responsible for her vindictiveness.

7. Decide Where You'll Live When You Separate – Will you keep the house and lose your spouse? Will she fight you tooth and nail for your home? If you are renting, who will move and who will stay?

8. Stay Connected With Your Kids – They'll need you more than ever during the tough times ahead. Think about the depth and quality of your relationship with them and do everything you can to enhance both. Divorce courts and judges consider these factors when assigning custody and visitation rights.

9. Consider the Differences Between Separation & Divorce – Check your state laws about the sometimes subtle differences between divorce and separation. Remember that the finality of divorce cannot be reversed. Legal separation, on the other hand, gives you both a breather and time to consider whether divorce is the right step. This is an important decision because nearly 20% of men regret divorcing their wives later. Make sure you are not one of them.

10. Decide How You'll Tell Your Wife & Kids – Obviously, you should tell your wife first. Think about the best time and place for such an announcement. Will she take it better in private or a public place? If you think she might flip out, consult a professional therapist before your announcement for advice about how best to handle her volatile reaction. Then decide whether you will tell your kids by yourself or together with your spouse. Be sensitive to timing, too. Don't break the news during a holiday such as Christmas, Thanksgiving, your anniversary, a child's birthday or some other personal special occasion.

11. Consider Your Life as an Unmarried Man – What will your life look and feel like when you are on your own? The best time to think about that is *before* you ask for a divorce.

12. Get a Second Opinion – If you're not sure you are doing the right thing for you, consult with a trusted friend, family member (e.g., a brother who has been married and divorced) or professional counselor.

Consider the odds. Statistics say there's a good chance your marriage will fail.

Knowing that, and knowing there's risk involved, you should take immediate action to protect yourself. That's why you buy homeowners or car insurance before you experience a catastrophe. You need to understand your risks and take steps to ensure that when divorce comes, it will be handled in a financially fair and emotionally reasonable manner.

Who Files for Divorce and Why?

Where children are involved, women file for almost 85% of divorces, according to the National Center for Health Statistics. That figure is up from 69% in 1975. Some experts believe it's because women with children have so much more to gain by instigating divorce, including the kids, house, car, dog, big-screen TV, child support and alimony. If so many more women are doing it, then they must have strong incentives.

They also get the control many women today seem to covet. They can legally "kidnap" their children by removing them from the home, or have the father removed from the home, or convince the father that a *trial* separation is best and coerce him into leaving her in charge of the children. After all, most of society believes the children belong with the mother.

That's why most fathers concede custody to mothers without argument. Then, to their horror, they later find out that they must pay thousands of dollars in legal fees and court costs just to get standard visitation rights. So unless you are financially prepared to fight to see your own children, *never concede custody until you have secured legal visitation rights!*

Keep in mind that few attorneys have ever won sole custody *for the father.* And few attorneys ever advise male clients the same way they advise female clients. The truth is, men can legally "kidnap" their children in the same ways as women and apply the same tactics for gaining custody as women. Yet, most men are unaware of it.

Women without children file for 75% of divorces in America. Again, could it be that they have so much more to gain?

You probably know men who are quite unhappily married yet hesitate to file for divorce because they believe they'll get killed financially. Perhaps *you* are one of those men. These feelings are well-founded and strongly supported by public records.

But instead of taking action that could improve your life dramatically, you do nothing and die a slow death, day by day. Or you procrastinate until *she* files and you get killed financially anyway. If you are unhappily married and your marriage is realistically beyond repair, the absolute best thing you can do for yourself is take the first step.

Don't wait for her to do it. Take control. File for divorce now.

The Myth of the Deadbeat Dad

What becomes of divorced men? Some will become dead-beat dads, though not nearly as many as the majority of people think. The truth is, well over half of all non-paying dads earn less than $6155 a year and are living well below the poverty line. They cannot afford support for their children any more than they can afford decent housing or groceries for themselves. In truth, most deadbeat dads are really dead-broke dads.

The majority of men in these circumstances are saddled with unrealistic child support obligations based not on real income but on something called "imputed" or suspected income. For example, a man earns $4,000 per month. The man's *girlfriend* earns $10,000 per month. Most courts today will calculate his child support obligation based on their belief that the man derives some benefit from his girlfriend. Child support obliga-tions in cases such as this often *exceed a man's actual personal income!*

The result: More and more men are being trapped in a debt cycle, only a fraction of which is caused by actual child support obligations. The massive, government-run legal system now tacks on many penalties and administrative fees that raise the amounts far beyond what is actually levied in child support orders. Recent statistics show that the average man pays almost $5,000 annually in child support alone.

The fact is, according to family court records, over 90% of fathers with joint custody pay the child support due. Nearly 80% of fathers with restricted visitation privileges pay the support due. Deadbeat dads are, far and away, the minority. In truth, men who lose custody are more reliable at paying child support than women who lose custody. Though far fewer women (less than 10%) lose custody battles, their numbers are still significant and they are far less likely than men to pay. According to public records, less than 40% of women who are ordered to pay child support actually pay.

Whether or not you have children and whether you are contemplating divorce, in the midst of a costly divorce or surviving after divorce, the simple message of this book is that there is hope. There is a better way.

Many of the opinions expressed here were spawned by the death of a 19-year marriage. The opinions apply mainly to one specific relationship and one female, not all relationships or all females.

I survived two divorces. The first was amicable and humane after five years of disagreements about everything, three separations and the final realization that we had nothing in common on which to build a lasting union. In the end, we both acted reasonably mature. We attempted to minimize the pain as much as the pain of a marital breakup can be minimized, especially because a child was involved.

My second divorce was fraught with drama (much like the marriage). In the end, it was destructive and insidious. With all trust, intimacy and respect gone from the relationship, we both acted despicably.

Both experiences provided important lessons.

The woman you married is just one woman, not all women.
Don't fall into the common trap of believing all women are bad just because the one you married was bad. If you have one bad meal, do you stop eating? If you have one bad day at work, do you quit working?

Your marriage is not all marriages.
Just because yours sucks doesn't mean they all suck.

You probably picked the wrong woman for you.

It happens to the best of us. Admit it. Showing poor judgment does not make you a bad person. It doesn't make you a failure and it doesn't make you any less of a man. It simply means you showed poor judgment in choosing a life partner.

The healthiest and most productive recourse is to figure out why your marriage failed, accept your share of responsibility for it, get over it, move on and embrace your new life. But that's the abbreviated and vastly oversimplified *Readers' Digest* version.

The rest of this book will give you the expanded version with nuts-and-bolts advice about surviving divorce with your health, sanity, sex life, spirit and finances intact. It will touch on issues that go to the heart of divorce; issues such as equality and the nature of men's and women's roles in America today.

I will also share some of the more poignant moments of my personal divorce story as they apply. You may identify with them. You may be in a similar situation right now. Either way, you may learn something from my experiences, as I did.

Except for a few of the more bizarre details, my story is probably not much different than a million other divorce stories. Unfortunately, many men have encountered women at their worst. What's important is what you learn from your experience and how you apply it to how well you fare as a human being and a man afterward.

PART ONE:

Surviving Before Divorce

*"Home life, as we understand it,
is no more natural to us than a cage
is natural to a cockatoo."*

– George Bernard Shaw, 1856-1950

Where the Rubber Meets the Road

Right now, whether you know it or not, the woman you promised to spend your life with may be plotting your untimely departure. She may be consulting attorneys, girlfriends, books, libraries and Internet sites to learn everything she can about the divorce laws and practices in your state and to determine what she can gain by divorcing you.

Four out of five married men don't have a clue that their wives are doing this until it's too late. With so many other things on their minds and virtual blinders on, most men miss the signs of trouble brewing in paradise, no matter how obvious they may be.

Many men, in fact, don't realize their marriage is in serious trouble until they are served with divorce papers. By then, it's too late. She already has everything orchestrated in her favor. And you don't have a leg to stand on or, potentially, a house to stand in.

Is Your Marriage in Trouble?

How do you recognize the signs that your marriage is in trouble?

First, instead of tuning her out as many men do (often with good reasons), pay closer attention to what your spouse is really saying and doing. And don't just listen. *Understand.* While men are usually straightforward and logical in their communication styles, women are usually circuitous and emotional.

Is she talking more or less than usual? Is she whining more or complaining that you don't communicate? Is she suddenly talking about "what ifs"? What if you were single again? What if you went to see a marriage counselor? What if things were different between you?

Pay attention to her schedule and her whereabouts. Have there been any changes lately? Is she doing anything differently? Does she jump when the home phone rings?

Has she taken up any new activities outside the home? Volunteer work. A college class. A part-time job. Tupperware parties. Is she suddenly more interested in the household finances or your investments? Has she been more distant lately?

Pay attention to her friends and family. Are they acting differently around you? Pay attention, but don't be obvious about it, unless you want to arouse her suspicions.

Ask her straight out if she is happy in the marriage. Then pay attention to her facial expressions, body language and tone of her answer. Does she make eye contact with you when she speaks?

Accept the fact that she might not answer you directly and truthfully. Keep in mind that women generally have different communication styles than men. And most women are rather adept at communicating indirectly and untruthfully.

Your wife might just as easily be cheating on you, too. According to statistics, more women are cheating now than ever before.

Either way, if you notice any of the telltale signs, don't wait. Do exactly what she would do (and may be doing at this very moment). Consult attorneys, friends, books, libraries and Internet sites. Learn everything you can about the divorce laws and practices in your state and try to determine exactly what she can take from you by divorcing you.

Make this a *high priority* because your kids, your house, your car, your dog and your furniture are all at stake, not to mention your health, finances, sanity and future. And remember that there are large variations in state law governing families and divorce. That's why it's critical that you learn about your state's laws and how they apply to you.

When it comes to divorce wars, the advantage almost always goes to the side that has the most knowledge, strikes first and uses the element of surprise. That's the side you want to be on. But, far more often than not, men are on the losing side and end up being taken to the cleaners in shock.

Are You Being Deceived?

"The cruelest lies are often told in silence."
– Adlai Stevenson, 1900-1965

When it comes to your divorce, your spouse may try to deceive you, her attorney and the court. My ex played her "poor-abandoned-unloved-woman" card to the hilt, not just with me but with all the attorneys she consulted and many of her acquaintances.

Most men, including attorneys, are clueless about an impending divorce until they receive the divorce papers from process servers. Process servers are people who work for attorneys and courts. Their job is to locate you, physically hand you the divorce summons and have you sign for it in their presence.

When it comes to surviving your divorce, truth will be your greatest ally. Because the only way you can overcome a spouse's deception is by uncovering the truth, then being able to prove it. Too many men give up at this point. They prefer to avoid confrontations with their spouses and take what seems like the easy way out.

This is a costly, stupid mistake.

With hundreds or thousands or millions of dollars and your financial future on the line, you have to disprove her deception by gathering evidence to the contrary. If you have to record her home phone conversations from an extension while she plans parties with her friends, or trysts with her boyfriend, do it. Round up witnesses who are willing to corroborate her shenanigans. Gather her phone bills, bank statements and credit card records, too. Be prepared to fight her deception with truth.

An angry, vindictive woman will do everything in her power to ruin you. So you must do everything in your power to protect yourself and your assets. Don't bury your head in the sand and hope everything will resolve itself in your favor, because it won't. In fact, it will cost you a fortune.

You don't just want to survive. You want to prevail. If you suspect that she is making moves for a split, shore up your finances. Shift as many of your assets as possible to trusted family members or friends for safekeeping until the divorce is final. If you have joint bank accounts or credit cards, separate them.

Attitude is everything.

If you think you somehow deserve to lose it all, you will probably end up losing it all. If you think separation or divorce will leave you lonely and depressed, you will probably end up lonely and depressed. If you're going to create self-fulfilling prophecies, make them positive and life-enhancing.

Don't believe everything your ex tells you about yourself.

In any conflict, she will do her best to make you feel smaller and less physically threatening. That's what women often do in arguments with larger, physically stronger male adversaries. They verbally cut you down to size in an attempt to level the playing field. They use facial expressions, body language and tone of voice to convince you, often in motherly tones, that you are wrong. Too often, bitchiness beats brawn.

My ex told me, for example, that I would be alone for the rest of my life because no other woman would ever want me. Like many statements she made, this one was off the mark.

Treat your separation as an opportunity for growth and rediscovery.

Learn to appreciate the little things and the joys they bring. Like watching sports without being told how stupid the game is or how stupid you are for watching it. Or leaving the toilet seat up. Like looking at another woman without guilt. Or seeing the action movie you want to see, instead of the chic flick she wants you to see.

You always choose your feelings.

This is difficult for most people to accept. They find it easier to blame how they feel at any given moment on someone or something else. If someone cuts you off on the freeway, you can get angry or you can ignore it and continue driving. Either way, you have chosen how you feel about being cut off and what being cut off means to you.

Did someone cut you off on purpose? Was it a personal attack or, more likely, was it just someone who was not paying attention?

Since it is unlikely that anyone is holding a gun to your head, which feelings will you choose for yourself?

Whether you are on the fence about your marriage or seriously contemplating divorce, remember there are many alternatives to being stuck in a dysfunctional marriage and they aren't all bad.

Besides, few men deserve to be miserable voluntarily. No one is forcing you to stay married. The rest of your life is waiting for you. The question is what are *you* waiting for?

Ask yourself if you are a better person with your spouse or without her.

Is she enhancing your life or sucking the joy from it? Is being together making you stronger as individuals or weaker? Does she make you feel good as a man or bad? Is being alone better for you than *wishing* you were alone?

Is Your Sex Life Dead or Dying?

According to the Foundation for Intimacy in Tampa, Florida, over 20 million American couples go to bed together every night but never have sex. Studies show that nearly half of all married couples engage in sex less than *once per week*. A third of all married couples have sex less than *four times per year!* At the other end of the marital sex spectrum, about 8 % of all couples engage in sex *four or more times per week*.

The statistics cut across all age groups. Even couples in their 20s and 30s are having sex less and less frequently these days. Psychologists say that the pace of American life has increased so much that most couples today are perpetually exhausted and have very little time or energy to enjoy true intimacy.

There's also a good deal of research revealing that a lack of sexual activity compromises male and female health and may even shorten life. For example, men who ejaculate less frequently are more likely to get prostate cancer. Women who have sex less often have weakened immune systems and are more likely to suffer from chronic illnesses.

Are you finding that your sex life is more about work than play? Do you only touch each other while in the bedroom? Have you stopped looking forward to sex or having sexual thoughts about your partner? Do you only have sex at fixed times (e.g., Saturday nights)? Has it become routine and mechanical? Are you the one who always initiates sex?

These are all signs of a less-than-healthy sex life. The fact is that most couples need regular sex to stay intimate and civil with each other. So how does your sex life stack up? Are you happy with it? Is she?

Should You Separate?

If you think your marriage is the reason for your unhappiness, try a separation. If you find that you are happier without her, consider divorce. If you find that you are still unhappy, consider that your marriage may not be the cause. Otherwise, you could end up like that one man in five who regrets getting divorced in the first place.

Other Divorce Questions You Must Answer

Now is the time to address other divorce questions if you haven't already done so.

How will you prepare for such practical considerations as family finances and your children?

How will you divide the marital assets?

How many children are involved and how old are they?

Whose children are they?

Who will get custody of the children?

Whom will the children want to live with?

What kind of financial and emotional support will they need?

What visitation rights will you want?

If you own a home, who will live in the home? Who will move out? Or will you sell the home, divide the profits and establish two new residences where you will both have less than you did as a couple?

If you are still on the fence about divorce, consider other options.

Have you tried counseling to save your marriage? The couples counseling industry has exploded in America since 1966, when, according to *Time*, there were only about 1,800 experts in the field. By 2001, that number had grown to over 47,000 practitioners counseling nearly 1 million couples each year.

For many couples, seeing a marriage counselor is a last-ditch remedy. Counseling cannot heal a sick, dysfunctional marriage, but it can help you move on through your inevitable separation as healthier individuals.

Today's new breed of counselors seems to prefer a more aggressive approach to saving marriages. They are less willing to advise divorce than their older predecessors were. Only time will tell whether they are achieving any greater success at keeping couples together.

Do-It-Yourself Divorce

Once you are headed for divorce, give serious consideration to the do-it-yourself type. A *pro se* (for yourself) divorce will save you thousands of dollars in attorney fees. But for a *pro se* divorce to work, you must agree to terms by negotiating directly with your spouse (not as easy as it sounds) and filing all the necessary paperwork with the court serving your area.

This paperwork should include complete financial disclosures from you and your spouse detailing all your assets and debts, and hers, as well as when assets were obtained and debts incurred. You will also include the specifics of the agreement you and your spouse negotiated. This should spell out, in detail, what property is to be divided and how, along with how much alimony and child support will be paid, when, to whom and for how long.

Some couples do it all themselves. Most of the necessary forms can be found online or at your local library or courthouse. Read the descriptions of the forms and check your state laws to find out which forms are required.

Do You Have Grounds?

Every state has different grounds (legal reasons) for divorce. These can vary from simple incompatibility to infidelity to physical and mental abuse.

In New York, for example, you can obtain a divorce on the grounds of losing your spouse's sexual services. Ironically, the legal term for this is *constructive abandonment*. If you're scratching your head and wondering what's constructive about it, join the club. Adultery (infidelity) is grounds for divorce in New York.

In California, you can cheat on your spouse with impunity. Infidelity is not grounds for divorce in California. Of course, you'll still risk the wrath of the woman you've scorned. She just can't divorce you for it. Before you start celebrating, remember that if she's like most women, she'll find other legal grounds to divorce you on. Check your state laws and statutes to be sure.

No-Fault and Default Divorces

About one-third of all states are now "no-fault" divorce states. This simply means that you don't have to have grounds, other than incompatibility, sometimes referred to as irreconcilable differences, to get divorced. If you live in one of these states, you will likely have an easier time obtaining a divorce.

If you decide not to respond to divorce papers served on you, your spouse can still obtain a divorce by default. Most states allow 20 to 30 days for a response, and some judges will make your spouse wait up to three months until a default divorce is granted, but a lack of response will not affect the outcome. Your failure to respond will not reduce the impact of divorce on your finances and responsibilities. You may still get taken to the cleaners.

Check your state laws to make sure you have all the facts before you proceed.

In 2001, there were 17 "pure" no-fault states, including Arizona, California, Colorado, Florida, Indiana, Iowa, Kansas, Kentucky, Michigan, Minnesota, Missouri, Montana, Nebraska, Oregon, Washington, Wisconsin and Wyoming. Two more no-fault states have options for separation with waiting periods: You must be separated one year in Nevada and two years in Hawaii before you can be granted a divorce.

There are 12 no-fault states that also have "fault options," or specific grounds, including Alaska, Delaware, Georgia, Maine, Massachusetts, Mississippi, New Hampshire, New Mexico, North Dakota, Oklahoma and South Dakota. In Tennessee, divorce due to separation cannot be used as a no-fault option if your children are living in that state.

Eight states (plus the District of Columbia) have different waiting periods before you can be granted a no-fault divorce.

The waiting periods vary from six months in Louisiana and the District of Columbia to one year in West Virginia, two years in Alabama and Pennsylvania and three years in Rhode Island, Texas and Utah. Idaho requires a five-year wait before you can obtain a no-fault divorce.

There are three states with no-fault "exceptions." Connecticut will grant a divorce after 18 months of separation only if incompatibility is alleged. Illinois allows no-fault divorce if "irretrievable breakdown and separation" is alleged. If there are objections from either spouse, then two years of separation are required. Otherwise the waiting period is only six months. Ohio law states that a no-fault divorce filing will be denied if one party contests the grounds of incompatibility. The waiting period for a divorce after separation is one year.

There are eight "fault" states that also permit divorce after legal separation and waiting periods of six months or more, such as Vermont (six months), Maryland, New York, North and South Carolina (one year) and Virginia (one year if there are children or six months without children). New Jersey and Arkansas have 18-month waiting periods.

All together, 42 states (plus the District of Columbia) allow no-fault divorces, some with options. There are only eight strictly "fault" states where specific grounds must be alleged and agreed to before a divorce can be granted. If you live in one of those states, you must be prepared to cite specific grounds for your divorce according to your state's laws.

Know Your State's Divorce Laws

With so many variations, it's important that you understand the divorce and child support laws in your home state as you enter negotiations. Under many states' laws, for example, all assets and debts acquired during marriage are divided equally between the divorcing parties. It is called "community property."

After you've studied your state's laws, start your negotiation by making an appointment with your spouse and setting your agenda and ground rules for the negotiations. You will need all your combined bank statements, earnings statements, W-2s, debts and expenses and assets such as stocks, IRAs and 401(k) and 403(b). Then, at the appointed time, with calculator and notebook in hand, begin negotiating.

The Three Most Critical Issues

According to legalzoom.com, a website that provides paper-work for those who choose to divorce without a lawyer, there are three key questions in every divorce.

1. How will community property be divided?

2. Who will have custody of the children?

3. How much child and spousal support should be paid?

No divorce is truly "uncontested" in the sense that there are no disagreements, but the disagreements do not always have to be resolved in court, either. An uncontested divorce is one where the spouses can agree to divorce terms without going to trial. Uncontested divorces move much faster through the court system and are much less expensive.

If you are seeking a divorce, you should first use all means possible to work out mutual terms with your wife for the separation and divorce without going to attorneys or court. If you and your wife cannot work things out, you should consider arbitration and mediation without attorney representation. This will save you time and money. By bypassing a lengthy litigation and trial process, an uncontested divorce typically leads to reduced hostility and resentment between you and your spouse. You will also be able to resume your life more quickly.

Contested divorces, on the other hand, often involve complex issues, high financial stakes and all kinds of technical-legal maneuvers in court. While an uncontested divorce can often be performed without an attorney, you may be forced to retain experienced counsel in a contested divorce due to the legal complexities involved. If your spouse is represented by an attorney, or if there are difficult or major financial issues involved in the divorce, you may be forced to seek an attorney to represent you. Having two attorneys on your family's payroll will be a very costly proposition – one you should try to avoid no matter what. Because every dollar you pay to attorneys is a dollar less for you, your spouse and your children.

Keep in mind that the difference between a herd of crazed rhinos and an attorney is that the attorney charges more.

Smart couples hire a legal service to prepare and file the papers for them. This service can cost from $300 to $600, or thousands less than hiring attorneys.

Check your state divorce laws to determine if you live in a "no-fault" divorce state. Some couples have moved to no-fault states just so they can obtain a divorce more easily. It may be sufficient in a no-fault state for you to claim incompatibility or irreconcilable differences leading to the final marital breakdown.

No matter which course you take once you've decided to split, your goal is to obtain your divorce as quickly and as inexpensively as possible.

Couples who have been married a short time and have no children or major assets to divide should always go the *pro se*, or "do-it-yourself," route. In marriages of up to three to five years, hiring attorneys is a complete waste of your money.

Even couples who have been married longer with children, homes, cars and other assets to divide would be wise to consider a *pro se* divorce. But they must be willing to negotiate fairly and divide their assets without the costly meddling of attorneys. And that challenge is simply too daunting for many men.

As difficult and painful as negotiating directly with your spouse may sound, it is still far better and far less costly than hiring attorneys. I consulted attorneys prior to both of my divorces and found, in both cases, that their fees would have nearly bankrupted me.

Given the choice between bankruptcy and negotiating head-to-head with your soon-to-be ex, chose direct negotiation.

Sleeping With the Enemy

"Marriage is the only war in which you sleep with the enemy."
– Francois, Duc de La Rochefoucauld, 1613-1680

Face it. When it comes to sex, women know that they control 100% of the world's vaginal assets. As long as they know that, they have a huge advantage over us.

That's why you should stop sleeping with your spouse now.

Sex will be her ultimate weapon until the moment you leave the marital bed. As long as you want sex, she has the upper hand in the relationship. Take that away and she'll be utterly disarmed by your sudden loss of sexual attention.

Not sleeping with her will give you a different perspective on the marriage. It may also give you hours of peaceful sleep every night, which will improve your ability to function during the day. You may start performing better at work.

During the last six months of our living together, I hardly exchanged words with my ex, much less physical intimacy. Her deceit (faking an illness) and criminal activities (fraud, passing bad checks, shoplifting) had affected me so profoundly, I found it difficult to be in the same room with her, much less the same bed. After 19 years of marriage, she had turned into a stranger, a criminal without conscience or remorse. Her daily regimen of Prozac, Xanax, Vicodin and Neurontin had turned her into a bloated, soulless, sexless, shoplifting robot.

Millions of women are taking these medications. Recent research has shown that women who are on Prozac and other antidepressants (Paxil, Zyban, Celexa, Zoloft and Lithium), also known as selective serotonin re-uptake inhibitors (SSRIs), can have underdeveloped sexuality, flattened moods and altered judgment. The experiences of many men married to women on SSRIs bear that out.

If your spouse is on SSRIs or other prescription medications, tread carefully and consider getting out of the relationship. You can be certain that the drugs will alter her brain chemistry, her feelings and her personality. Some of the changes will be subtle and some will be obvious. Pay attention to her moods and actions.

Never sleep with anyone who's out to get you.

My ex kept telling me about a recurring dream in which she stabbed me repeatedly with a butcher knife while I slept. She loved telling me this. After that, I started locking myself in my home office to protect myself from her. I slept on the floor in a sleeping bag (we couldn't afford a spare bed) with the doors and windows locked for nearly two months.

It doesn't matter how horny you are. It won't kill you to abstain from sex for a while. If you are like most married men, you're probably not having sex frequently enough, anyway. Despite that, some men are gluttons for punishment. Some men will do anything for sex. Some men even get killed for it. They have sex with someone else's wife or girlfriend and get caught in the act, beat up, stabbed or shot. It happens every day in America.

Don't let your sex drive control you.

You can find sexual satisfaction without subjecting yourself to an angry or vindictive partner. Instead of sleeping with the enemy, sleep alone in another room and live to tell your buddies about it.

Real Men Don't Leave

"He knows not his own strength that hath not met diversity."
— Ben Jonson, 1573-1637

Every year in America, hundreds of thousands of married men give up their security and leave home not by choice but by circumstances. In most cases, they will only get to see their homes on weekends thereafter, and just long enough to pick up or drop off their children for scheduled visitation.

Sadly, most men in this predicament are *still* paying for the homes they are legally barred from living in. So what's the alternative?

No matter how bad things get at home, do not leave.

Do not stay with friends or relatives or sleep in your car.

If she refuses to leave, too, then wait her out.

You've probably heard that "possession is nine tenths of the law." In divorce, possession is everything. If you walk out, you will find it almost impossible to get back in.

Your home is the biggest and possibly the best investment you'll ever make. As long as you stay, you have a chance of keeping it. By staying, you have a fighting chance of getting her out. Instead of following the path of least resistance and leaving, gut it out and fight to keep what you have most likely bought and paid for.

Stay in your home and you'll have a much better chance of keeping it.

The Thrill is Gone

"Nothing great was ever achieved without enthusiasm."
— Ralph Waldo Emerson, 1803-1882

Once you've decided that the thrill has gone out of your marriage, do yourself the ultimate man's favor. As Arnold Schwarzenegger says, *"Get out."* Get out of the marriage while you still have your sanity and what's left of your money.

My second marriage died years before I buried it. Instead of admitting failure and cutting my losses, I hung in there, like a cat caught in the curtains, trying to make it work. It was a bad move financially and emotionally. As it turned out, waiting just two more years cost me well over $50,000. During this time, my spirit died a little more each day.

Don't kid yourself.

If the bad outweighs the good, get out. If you aren't sure, grab a sheet of paper, draw a line down the middle and list the good and the bad. Use cold, calculating logic to determine what is good and bad about your marriage. And keep in mind that the longer you stay in the relationship, the more costly your divorce will likely be and the longer you will have to pay alimony or support. In fact, you may have to pay six months more support for each year you prolong the inevitable.

Life is way too short to be miserable voluntarily. Don't wait for lightning to strike or a sudden, miraculous change for the better. It won't happen. GET OUT NOW!

Do You Believe in Black Magic?

"When you have eliminated the impossible,
whatever remains, however improbable, must be the truth."
– Arthur Conan Doyle, 1859-1930

True story: I didn't believe in black magic until my ex got into it with her creepy girlfriend. They were casting spells and putting hexes on me, chanting and drawing pentagrams on the floor. They were making my hair stand on end.

One night, I was awakened at 4 a.m. by strange guttural sounds coming from upstairs. I was sleeping in my office. The sound wafted right down from the loft to the living room and into the room where I slept on the floor.

My ex was speaking in a voice I barely recognized. But she wasn't talking on the phone and her creepy girlfriend hadn't shown up in the middle of the night.

I slipped quietly from my sleeping bag and crept into the living room. I picked up the extension phone and heard only a dial tone. Then I heard a soft mechanical whirring sound. It was oddly familiar. So was the mechanical giggle that followed. Then, I heard my ex again.

She was talking to her Furby. Furby was a popular child's toy that year. It looked like something from the movie *Gremlins*. My ex was 45 years old. She spoke to the Furby as if she was training a child. It was blood-chilling. I thought I had awakened in an insane asylum.

That's what a bad marriage feels like. Maybe that's why they call marriage an "institution" and use words such as "committed" to describe it.

If you find yourself living with this or some other kind of insanity, get off the fence and get out of the relationship.

The Grass Isn't Always Greener

You're driving home from work one day in rush-hour traffic when you happen to glance across the median at a car being driven by a blonde California beach babe type. You are creeping along at 5 mph. She's a major head-turner. Tight, toned and tanned. She has an angelic face most guys would die for.

Then, just as your little fantasy starts to get interesting, this 20-something hottie pokes her head out the window and spits. It's not some gentle little girlie spit, either. It's a big, honking, nasty green loogie she launches forcefully right into the concrete median. Your bikini beach fantasy dissolves in that instant, only to be replaced by this thought: For every beautiful woman you see, there's probably a man who is sick of her. He might even be sick of having sex with her.

At a recent party, I ran into an old friend and his stunning, raven-haired young wife. They'd been married five years and seemed perfectly happy together. As soon as she was beyond earshot, I complimented him on his good taste and great fortune. He grinned knowingly, then leaned over and said, "Don't be fooled by her looks. She's a high-maintenance bitch who flirts with my friends and spends all my money on herself."

**Judging a woman by physical beauty alone
is a common male mistake.**

We all have different definitions of beauty. One thing we can agree on is that physical beauty fades over time. And in the end, that hot-looking "trophy" wife often turns into something less than a trophy. It's called a "booby prize." Besides, you never really know a woman until you have lived with her. Or spotted her spitting on the freeway. Or faced off against her in a divorce case.

PART TWO:

Surviving During Divorce

*"The first blow
is half the battle."*

– Oliver Goldsmith, 1728-1774

Living on a Prayer

Don't wait for the divorce proceedings to get underway before you get a handle on your personal credit and finances. As soon as you realize that your marriage is headed south, take stock of all the credit cards and accounts you and your future ex have been sharing.

This is a good time to send for your credit report. It gives you a current snapshot of your total credit picture. Sometimes your own bank or another lending institution will send you the report free. You can also look for free offers in the mail. I usually get two or three each year.

But the best way to access your credit report free is on the web. Under federal law, you can obtain a free credit report online according to your state of residence. Your free online report will provide credit information from the three reporting agencies, Equifax, Experian and Trans Union. This free program began with the Western states in December of 2004. By September of 2005, men from coast to coast will have access to their free annual credit reports by pointing their browsers (the program you use to access the Internet) at this website: https://www.annualcreditreport.com/cra/index.jsp.

Once you receive your report, study it carefully. Correct any errors you find by writing to the creditor (the company you owe money to). Send proof of the error along with your cover letter describing it clearly. Your resulting corrected credit report will tell you where you stand right now.

You should also have at least one major credit card in your own name – one that you don't share with her. Remember that a wife can readily use her husband's credit card without raising a merchant's eyebrow, as long as she can prove she's the wife (and sometimes, they don't even ask for such proof!).

But try using one of her credit cards in the same way. You cannot without her written permission, even if you can prove you're the husband.

Separate all your assets, credit and debt into three categories: yours, hers and what you have combined. Then take steps to eliminate as many of your joint accounts as possible. This is a divide-and-conquer strategy.

If you are lucky, your ex's free-spending ways won't impact your credit. If your credit report arrives clean, count your blessings. Open a checking account in your name and have your name removed from your joint account. Let it be hers alone. Do the same with credit cards you hold jointly.

You can also quietly remove her as the beneficiary on any life insurance policies, though most attorneys and counselors advise against this. Ideally, by the time you negotiate your divorce, you should have very few jointly held assets left to bicker over.

Love is a Battlefield

*"Courage is the art of being the only one who knows
you're scared to death."*
– Harold Wilson, Baron of Rievaulx, 1916-1995

If you are like many couples, you will fight to the bitter end. An excellent example of this is in the movie *War of the Roses*. But there are ways to diffuse even the nastiest divorce battles without causing each other physical harm. Divorce wars can take many prisoners as both sides rape, pillage and plunder each other and any innocent bystanders who happen to get in the way – children, family members, friends and co-workers.

There are ways to diffuse your anger and hers, but you need a clear head if you want a peaceful resolution. Of course, that is more easily said than done in the heat of a matrimonial war. Here are ten simple strategies to use when skirmishes break out.

One: Stop what you are doing and give your motor a chance to wind down.

Two: Close your eyes. Take five or six long, slow deep breaths. This will help you relax your muscles and get oxygen to your brain so you can think clearly.

Three: Think before you say anything. Winning the divorce wars takes brainpower and willpower, not firepower. Focus on the outcome and ask yourself if your words or actions will give you the result you want.

Four: Separate and define the issues at hand. Your motto here is "Divide and conquer."

Five: Timing is everything. If she's distracted by some other activity, wait until you have her undivided attention.

Six: Offer an olive branch (this could be an apology for losing your temper or some other peace offer) on her turf. Talk in a room where she feels comfortable. Show your willingness to sacrifice false pride in exchange for real peace.

Seven: Listen to her. If you don't understand her message, ask for clarification.

Eight: Speak calmly without raising your voice. Don't sound like a parent scolding a child and don't make wild accusations. Keep your tone simple, unemotional and honest.

Nine: Stick to the issues and make your feelings known. Remind her that fairness is in everyone's best interests and your goal is a peaceful resolution.

Ten: Accept your fair share of the blame. Neither of you is 100% innocent or 100% guilty.

Keep in mind men and women are raised and socialized differently. Men are goal-oriented and tend to think and react logically. Women are process-oriented and tend to feel rather than think. They react emotionally. You need to understand these essential differences if you want to communicate with her effectively.

When negotiating the divorce agreement with your spouse, be prepared to compromise. Be flexible, but stick to the issues. Avoid letting emotions such as anger, resentment or jealousy get in the way of a settlement. Emotions can be very costly to both sides in a divorce. If you feel a surge of emotion surfacing, back off. You need your male logic now more than ever.

Count to ten. Take a few deep breaths. Stop and ask yourself if your anger is really worth tens of thousands of dollars in legal fees once the lawyers get involved. Face the reality that you will both probably feel somewhat dissatisfied with your final agreement.

If you have negotiated fairly, you will both get a little less than you hoped for simply because you are turning one household into two. The economic reality is that you cannot and will not, except in rare circumstances where great wealth is involved, maintain the same standard of living you enjoyed as a couple.

Divorce Mediation or Arbitration

If you simply cannot agree, consider mediation. It's a relatively inexpensive alternative to hiring attorneys. Divorce mediators may be social workers or people who have received special certifications in divorce mediation. They will sit with you and your spouse, hear your issues, explain the applicable divorce laws in your state, suggest solutions to your disputes and help you reach a fair settlement.

Mediators can help you settle child custody, child support, visitation issues, alimony and property settlement issues. They can help you reach a legally binding marital settlement or divorce agreement without attorneys. Mediation works best when both parties want the divorce, know their assets and debts and can communicate fairly and flexibly.

To find a qualified mediation service, ask friends and acquaintances, check your local phone directory or call the local bar association. Mediators generally have degrees in psychology, social work or marriage/family counseling. Always ask for a list of references before selecting a mediation service. Then check the references to be sure.

Another alternative is arbitration. Don't confuse this with mediation. The two are very different processes. In arbitration, you and your spouse *and attorneys* go before an arbitrator to make your respective cases. After hearing both sides, the arbitrator makes a binding decision that cannot be appealed.

Dealing With Your Anger

You may feel a certain amount of anger or animosity toward your ex or soon-to-be ex. This is normal. What's important is how you choose to deal with it.

I felt extreme anger toward my ex because she had treated me poorly and deceived me during the last five years of our marriage into believing she was "disabled." Despite all my soul-searching, I could not find any justification for her abusiveness.

I didn't cheat. I didn't beat. I wasn't abusive, controlling or demanding.

Instead, I was a devoted caregiver for over four years after she became "ill." I waited on her. I stayed with her around the clock until her mounting medical bills pushed me back into a full-time job outside the home. Then I took time off to drive her to countless medical appointments. I fought for her disability benefits and won against incredible odds. I even researched and wrote a book about her controversial illnesses, chronic fatigue syndrome and fibromyalgia. Most of the doctors we encountered either didn't believe in them, couldn't or wouldn't diagnose them or didn't know anything about them whatsoever.

Though I was researching treatments and interviewing dozens of medical professionals – physicians, physical therapists, massage therapists and alternative medicine specialists – in an attempt to help her, I began to get suspicious because she systematically ignored my advice.

It took me a long time to see that *she didn't want to get better.*

I couldn't figure out why she was so verbally and mentally abusive. Or why the more I tried to help her, the more abusive she became.

Mainly, I didn't know that she was *faking her illness* so she wouldn't have to work, that she had played me like a violin for five years or that she had premeditated and plotted this entire melodrama. It wasn't until later that I learned the truth about her deception.

Is There a Best Time to Announce You Want a Divorce?

"Serious things cannot be understood without laughable things, nor opposites at all without opposites."
– Plato, c. 428-348 B.C.

After a long heart-to-heart talk, my ex and I decided to take a vacation together and try to reconnect as a couple. We thought there was a chance we could work things out in one last-ditch attempt to save the marriage. She was home all the time, so she made the travel arrangements.

Home life was relatively peaceful for several days until the tickets and luggage tags arrived. To my horror, there were *three sets* instead of two. She had invited her creepy girlfriend to join us on vacation – *the vacation that was supposed to save our marriage!*

Instead of reconnecting as a couple, we would be traveling as a trio.

Four weeks later, we boarded a plane to Mexico. We arrived two hours later and were shuttled to our destination on the Sea of Cortez.

As soon as we arrived at the resort, the women dropped seven pieces of luggage at my feet and went off to the gift shop, leaving me to confirm room assignments and transport their luggage to our respective rooms. When they returned two hours later, they were laughing about the leather sandals they had *stolen* from the gift shop. I was tempted to turn them in to the Mexican authorities.

It was the last straw.

Right there in the middle of a beautiful tropical resort, I told her I wanted a divorce and she was free to do as she pleased the rest of the week. After 19 years of marriage and 22 years together, we split up on our first night of vacation.

There is no such thing as a best time for divorce. You may want to avoid major holidays or family birthdays. Otherwise, anytime is a good time.

Or, to put it a different way, the best time to announce that you want a divorce is when you decide that the time is right. Even if it is on the first night of your vacation.

The Color of Money

"Of all the icy blasts that blow on love,
a request for money is the most chilling…"
– Gustave Flaubert, 1821-1880

Before you initiate divorce or try to negotiate a settlement with your soon-to-be ex, make sure you have all your financial ducks in a row. Make a list of every line item in the family budget. Include every expense, every debt and every asset you have. When you're done, repeat the process to make sure you haven't missed anything.

If your accounting and money management skills are lacking, consult a trusted friend who has those skills. If your spouse has been handling the family finances, ask to see her accounting records before the negotiations begin. If she balks, do whatever is necessary, short of breaking the law, to gain access to the information.

Leave nothing to chance. It's easy to overlook important bits of information when your emotions are involved. If ever there was a time for cold, clinical, unemotional calculation on your part, this is it. If you miss something in your calculations, it could cost you a great deal of money.

When calculating my own settlement, for example, I overlooked a $15,000 personal loan from my family that was used as a down payment on our condo. Despite my ex's opinion to the contrary ("Why should we repay them? They don't need the money."), we were morally and legally bound to repay the loan. But I overlooked this rather sizeable debt in my calculations – an oversight that cost me $7,500.

Is your spouse hiding assets? Divorcing spouses often find devious ways to hide money and other assets. Many even declare bankruptcy in the middle of their divorce. If your spouse does this to you, you may need a bankruptcy attorney to have the judge exclude you from the list of creditors who will not be paid. If your spouse declares bankruptcy, you can also challenge the decision.

Another popular deception is the illegal transfer. This is where a spouse transfers cash or other assets to friends or family members and claims she no longer has those assets. If you suspect this ploy, you may need the help of a lawyer or private investigator to uncover the truth. When this happens, the lawyer has to prove that a transfer was made and demonstrate that it was made in order to deprive you of your share of those assets.

To help you avoid any oversights, here's a beginning list of items you should consider as you negotiate your settlement:

Home
Other Real Estate
Business
Car Payments, Fuel Costs, Maintenance, Repairs
Boat Payments, Fuel Costs, Maintenance, Repairs
Savings
Checking
Pension(s)
IRA, 401(k), 403(b)
Bank CD(s)
Stocks, Bonds, Mutual Funds, Commodities
Clothing
Collectibles, Art, Antiques
Jewelry
Furnishings
Electronics

Auto, Life, Health, Homeowners, Dental Insurance
Credit Card Debt
Personal Debts
Outstanding Loans, Interest
Federal, State, Local Taxes
Salaries, Bonuses, Commissions
Other Income Sources
Utilities (Gas, Electric, Water, Waste Removal)
Telephone
Cable TV
Laundry
Internet
Professional Fees (attorneys, accountants, marriage counselors, etc.)
Medical Expenses
Dental Expenses
Memberships
Groceries
Dining Out
Pets, Pet Food, Vet Expenses, Licenses
Education Costs
Childcare, Daycare

This list is by no means complete. As you look at each of these items, you will think of others. Everything you acquired as a couple – assets and debts – must be counted in order to reach a fair settlement. Dollar values must be placed on everything.

Which brings up the subject of "wants vs. needs" and your ability to distinguish between the two. Needs are basics such as food, shelter, clothing, transportation, electricity, gas and a phone. Everything else pretty much falls into the "wants" category. Add up all your needs first and determine if there is enough income to cover those.

This process may make you sick. But hiring attorneys to control this process will make you a lot sicker, especially when you see their price tag.

There are other important financial decisions to be made if you hope to negotiate and reach a fair settlement. Here are some things to consider as you head toward divorce, including information about prenuptial (in case you have one) and postnuptial (in case you need one) agreements.

Postnuptial and Prenuptial Agreements

Though many people would argue the point, it's not unromantic for couples to consider postnuptial agreements any more than prenuptial agreements. Practically speaking, the best time to consider a worst-case scenario is when love is at its best. The best time to think about a car crashing into your house is the day you move in, when it's all fresh and new. A prenuptial may be valuable even if neither party is risking many assets going into the marriage, because, in time, those assets can grow. Greed can grow, too.

If you created a valid prenuptial agreement, you and your spouse must have been represented by separate attorneys. If you were smart, you found attorneys who worked for a reasonable flat fee. You must also have fully disclosed all assets. If your agreement specifies that those assets are to be kept separate, you may have placed them in a revocable living trust to protect them.

What about assets acquired during the marriage? How will those assets be distributed in the event of a divorce? Your prenuptial should also have spelled out your agreement to specific terms of financial support in the event of a divorce. Your agreement should also be designed to protect your assets at death so they can be distributed to any children from previous marriages. Both parties should also have created individual wills and estate plans to carry out their agreements.

Of course, if you didn't create a prenuptial before you married but wish you had one now, it's still not too late. The same type of agreement can be created and signed *during* marriage. This is called a *postnuptial* agreement. If you think your spouse would never consider such an arrangement, then read on.

Let's say your spouse has no work history or lacks the skills to support a reasonable lifestyle on her own (rare among women today), or she has young children to raise. These are considered *special circumstances* in the eyes of the law. Special circumstances can work against you in divorce because the law perceives your spouse to be at a disadvantage.

In these circumstances, it is highly unlikely she would sign a postnuptial agreement. And despite what most attorneys will tell you to the contrary, there is nothing romantic about asking a spouse to sign a "postnup." She will most likely act as if you slapped her face.

Dividing Property Fairly

So what other options do you have for reaching a fair division of property?

Unlike attorneys, financial planners, mediators and even insurance agents can add long-term value to your divorce if you use them properly. Their advice can actually shorten your divorce battle and save you the money you would otherwise pay attorneys to contest these issues and run up your tab.

A financial planner can make it easier to determine what's really fair in your divorce settlement. For example, if your house is worth $300,000 and you have the same amount in your retirement account, it may not be fair to give the house to your spouse so she can raise the children there. The house and retirement may have the same value now, but the house will need ongoing repairs, and home ownership exposes the owner to rising tax payments, repairs and utility bills. The house may appreciate in value, but there are ongoing maintenance costs attached. At the same time, a retirement plan will enjoy tax-deferred gains with no maintenance required.

Then there's health insurance. This can be one of the most important yet overlooked issues in divorce. It's an issue many men overlook in their calculations. If the family has used your insurance plan at work, your spouse may be left without health coverage after divorce.

You may still cover children on your company plan, as long as you can legally claim them as dependents for income tax purposes on your tax return. That will also be a point of contention during your negotiations. You will have to decide who gets to claim the kids on their income tax returns.

Does your spouse have a medical condition? Divorcing a spouse with a pre-existing medical condition may make it difficult and extremely expensive to get coverage for that condition. If your spouse has a medical condition that requires frequent or ongoing care, a separate policy in her name will save you from financial disaster. It may cost upwards of $500 or more a month, but one major surgery can cost tens of thousands if you don't have health insurance.

When you consider the potential cost of a catastrophic uncovered illness, or coverage for a medical condition such as cancer, it might affect your opinion of the divorce. So don't overlook health insurance when negotiating your settlement.

Dividing Your Retirement Plans and Insurance Policies

Another consideration is retirement plans – yours and hers, if she has one. Depending on your states laws, the assets of a 401(k), 403(b), IRA or pension plan may also be divided as part of your settlement. If you end up in court, the judge will issue something called a Qualified Domestic Relations Order, or QDRO. A QDRO instructs your retirement plan to separate any assets earmarked for your spouse until you reach retirement age. However, getting such an order enforced – especially if one spouse is covered by a municipal, state or union pension plan – may prove difficult.

If the working spouse is under age 59-1/2, any distribution of assets will incur a tax penalty. Your spouse typically does not have any voice in the investment of the 401(k), 403(b) or IRA assets.

Sometimes men or women insure part of the divorce agreement with a life insurance policy. For example, if you promise to pay college tuition for your children, the court may order you to carry enough life insurance to back your agreement in the event of your death. A good financial planner can help you calculate the rising cost of college for your children, so you can purchase adequate insurance to fulfill your obligation.

If you are required to buy life insurance, your wife will want to own the policy. That allows her to make sure the premiums are paid, but it also keeps you from changing the beneficiary or dumping her from the policy.

These are a few of the issues that can be easily overlooked in the heat of a divorce battle as attorneys are running up their tabs. Getting angry is the worst way to get even.

Getting angry will just about guarantee that you will both lose, while your attorneys eat up money that would be better spent for the children's benefit, or your benefit.

Using insurance agents, financial planners and qualified mediators will help you reach a financial settlement that you can both live with.

Divorce Has Become Big Business

The average total cost of divorce in America is about $15,000 per couple. And as the rate of broken marriages has become dauntingly high, divorce has become big business. Couples who once put their separation almost entirely in the hands of an attorney now often turn to a team of advisers to ensure a fair deal.

Arbitrators and mediators can be helpful. So can psychologists, particularly when children are involved. But money is always a key issue when your partnership breaks down. And that's where divorce financial analysts come in.

Divorce is a very angry, terrifying time for most people because they fear the unknown. Taking the financial unknown and putting it down on paper will help reduce your stress. Remember that divorce planners do not, as the name implies, help you plan your divorce. Instead, they help you secure your financial future after the marriage ends.

Divorce planners or divorce financial analysts aren't cheap. They usually charge $125 to $200 an hour for their help and work with you for several hours (still better than attorneys). Since the late 1980s, divorce planners have grown in popularity. There are now over 1,800 divorce planners in the United States.

According to the Institute for Divorce Financial Analysts, CPAs and other financial experts take a four- to six-month course to become certified divorce financial analysts. If you follow this route, ask your accountant, or any accountant – they're listed in the Yellow Pages – to refer you to one.

Your expenses, income(s), investments, child support, alimony, retirement, tax liability, inflation and other data will be plugged into complicated spreadsheets that help your divorce planner determine if your settlement is sensible and equitable for the years after your divorce. They know emotional turmoil cannot be avoided during a breakup, so they'll generally counsel you to accept your pain while you gain a clear understanding of the numbers. They might be able to help you reach a fairer settlement. Every decision you make today will impact your life later on.

Many of the divorces in America are handled *pro se* (without attorney representation) during a vulnerable time when your emotional attachments can wreak financial havoc. Even the best-intentioned settlement can leave you desperate and broke. That's why it helps to understand how divorce planners level your financial playing field:

One guy I know proposed a settlement in which his spouse kept the house, worth $265,000, and received $95,000 from his retirement plan. This guy took the $200,000 remaining in his IRA and 401(k). On top of that, he offered to pay his spouse a $1,200 monthly alimony for five years and $300 in monthly child support.

He though it was more than fair. But a forecasting graphic showed her net worth dropping to zero ten years after the divorce while his net worth skyrocketed. His settlement failed to consider the future.

The divorce financial analyst's spreadsheet showed that the spouse's expenses would eventually exceed her income and she would have to liquidate her portion of the retirement money to meet her expenses. Withdrawing those dollars early would mean additional taxes and penalty fees that would deplete most of the fund.

A second forecast showed that, if he paid alimony for ten years, she would stay afloat without dipping into the retirement money or reducing *his* net worth.

Keep this in mind when you bring a divorce financial analyst into the picture. It could cost you more than just their hourly fee. The smartest advice would be to run your *pro se* divorce agreement by your accountant to see if it makes sense for *you*. Do this on your own without disclosing it to her. If she hasn't thought about consulting a divorce financial analyst, why plant that thought in her head?

Statistics show that three out of four men believe divorce settlements favor women, while seven of ten women believe they favor men. Oddly enough, these numbers are almost identical. They underscore the fact that almost no one feels as though they come out ahead in a divorce.

Terms of Estrangement:
Alimony, Maintenance or Support

*"Experience is what you get
when you didn't get what you wanted."*
– Italian proverb

This is about what used to be called alimony and is now called maintenance or spousal support. These new terms attempt to remove the social sting of "alimony" and absolutely bristle with political correctness. Maintenance, after all, sounds like something you regularly do to your car. It's a man-friendly term for something that is anything but. And spousal support sounds like pure, cold-blooded legalese.

No matter what you call it (some men have suggested it be called "ransom"), it's a sum of money paid (to her) for the release of a prisoner (you). Do you have to pay it? Does she have to pay it? How much will have to be paid? How long will you have to pay?

On the upside, support is usually tax-deductible for the payer (child support is not), and must usually be claimed as income by the payee (child support does not). But that won't matter much if you can't afford groceries after your divorce. So think of ways to reduce or eliminate your support amount.

Let's say you earn $40,000 a year and she earns $20,000. The combined income equals $60,000. In a community property state and with all the other financial factors being equal, each of the spouses would receive about half the total. The $40,000 spouse (most often the man) would have to fork over about $10,000 to the $20,000 spouse (most often the woman) to even things out at $30,000 each. That's $833.33 a month in maintenance payments.

If you earn $40,000 and she earns $10,000, your combined income is $50,000. Each of you would end up with $25,000. Your maintenance cost in most community property states would be $15,000, or $1,250 every month.

You can reduce this by negotiating. Are you taking on a greater debt burden than your spouse? Do you have work-related or business-related expenses she does not have? Will you have moving costs because you are leaving the family home? Each of these line items must be considered when negotiating your settlement. You may also be able to negotiate a lump-sum settlement in lieu of the monthly alimony check. For many men, paying a lump sum is preferable to ongoing monthly checks – reminders of their failed marriage that also keep them connected, at least financially, to their ex.

Try everything. After all, it's your financial future at stake.

In addition to your incomes, the length of your marriage is often considered. If you both work full-time and you've only been married a few years, you may not have to pay support at all. For longer-term marriages, you may not be so lucky. If your spouse does not work, you will likely have to pay her to continue not working, at least for the foreseeable future. But there is hope.

Some states place a time limit on your support payments. They prefer to have your spouse return to the workforce after a period of adjustment, education and/or job training. The time limit may or may not relate to the length of your marriage. In other states, you have to pay support until you die, unless she remarries and becomes someone else's financial burden.

I was extremely lucky. My ex remarried quickly. My support payments only lasted seven months. Here's how they ended…

Soon after I received my copy of the final divorce decree, my ex left me a voicemail at work. She wanted me to send her next alimony payment two weeks earlier than usual. Instead of calling her back, I got suspicious. I knew that she was seriously involved and likely living with a man 3,000 miles away.

My suspicion led me, on a Friday the 13th, to the Internet for some research. I found the county in which they resided, located its public records website and navigated straight to the marriage license section. A search under their last names revealed they were married just 16 days after our divorce was final. Her urgent plea for an early alimony payment had occurred *eight days after she was remarried*! In addition to her other criminal acts, she had tried to collect alimony fraudulently.

Most guys would have called and given her a piece of their mind. I did something infinitely more satisfying. I printed a copy of *her new marriage license*, folded it neatly and placed it in the same envelope I used to mail her alimony checks. I added a short note congratulating her on her recent nuptials and mailed it to her.

In the course of a few hours on that memorable Friday the 13th, I stopped her support payments, cut off her insurance policies and saved myself over $1,400 in monthly payments. I reclaimed all of my income except the $380 monthly payment on the second mortgage I'd used to buy out her interest in the condo.

Which brings me to another caution regarding alimony:

Make sure your agreement states that alimony will cease immediately when your spouse remarries.

If you don't, she may still legally collect from you under certain conditions in some states. Check your own state's laws regarding alimony online or through the local library.

Don't assume that alimony payments stop automatically when your ex remarries.

Child Support

Child support is a different matter entirely.

Child support is usually a percentage of your income. It is usually based on the court's perception of the child's needs (based on the often biased or erroneous information provided by your spouse and her attorney), a percentage of your income or a combination of both. In most states, you are required to pay child support until your child reaches the "age of majority," or the legal age at which your state considers children adults. In most states, that's 18 (e.g., California) or 21 (e.g., New York). In some states, you pay only until the child is emancipated. If a child joins the military or moves out on his or her own, then he or she is legally emancipated, regardless of age.

My daughter left home at 19 and went out on her own. I stopped making support payments, even though she had not reached the age of majority in New York. Had she stayed home, I would have been required to pay two more years of support.

Review your state laws regarding child support.

There is a great deal of variation in statutes, depending on where you live. Most states have official websites where you may be able to obtain this information quickly and easily. If you can't get online, your local library is the next best thing.

In some cases, even nonbiological fathers can be forced to pay child support.

If you marry a woman who has children from a previous marriage, then divorce her, you may be forced to pay support for her children. Pay support for children who are not yours? Absurd, right? But it happens every day in America. If you're in this situation, check your state's laws and ask lots of questions.

Knowledge is power.

The more you know, the more effective you will be at negotiating with your soon-to-be ex. Take advantage of the free consultations offered by many attorneys. Use your time with them to learn as much as you possibly can about your legal rights and responsibilities.

If your spouse *earns more* than you, then *you* can collect spousal support or maintenance *from her!* If you are fortunate enough to be in that position (approximately 15% of men, or one in six, earn less than their spouses), you have a choice to make. If you accept her support, you could be buying into the same victim mentality that women often use. On the other hand, you may relish the idea of turning the tables on a woman who deserves it. Just keep in mind that *less than one percent* of men ever receive support from their spouses.

Men Are Being Enslaved

Today, millions of men live in virtual slavery created by the massive divorce/child support/paternity industries. Women truly have "power over" these men. Wives can sue for divorce with impunity secure in the knowledge that their husbands will be forced by governmental bureaucracy to fork over a large percentage of their income because it's in "the bests interests of the children."

Add this to the fact that men suffer the vast majority of injuries and deaths from war, crime, suicide and high-risk work, yet women get the vast majority of the healthcare dollars, including the bulk of the research and prevention money. There are over four times more suicides among men than women and men die seven years sooner, on average, regardless of the cause. The result: Social Security and inheritance have become primarily retirement programs for women.

Men and Paternity Fraud

Conservative estimates based on court and paternity records show there are now 10 million men indentured by paternity fraud under draconian court orders from which they cannot escape. These men have committed no crime, nor have they been convicted.

Government and courts throughout America have turned their backs on men, particularly fathers. Yet, surprisingly, many men are sympathetic to the feminist ideologies upon which our legal structures have been built.

Such pro-feminist male sympathizers don't study or understand the issues. They find it easier to "go along" rather than risk their ex's scorn. All they know is that if she's unhappy, everyone around her, including him, will be unhappy, too.

Are They Really Your Kids?

Children must be supported, and those who are not often drift to the destructive side of society. Contrary to the myths that abound in our society, few fathers actually abandon their own children. Even after a divorce they did not initiate, and did not want, most fathers care enough to provide for their kids. However, in the aftermath of a bitter divorce, many men resent paying for the care of children that their vindictive wives prevent them from seeing. Fatherhood for these men has become all responsibilities and no rights.

There are also too many cases of paternity fraud. All too often, the man the mother claims is the father is not, according to paternity records. The law does not acknowledge this fact and continues to extract a significant portion of men's incomes to go toward the support of children with whom they have no biological relationship.

Add to this the fact that approximately 80% of court-ordered paternity judgments are gained by default because the "father" is never notified that a judgment is pending against him. By the time he discovers this, the statute of limitations on challenging paternity has passed and he has no legal recourse.

According to a recent study that received widespread media attention, 30% of DNA paternity tests prove that the man named is not the father of the child in question. Currently, more than 300,000 paternity tests are done each year. And 90,000 men are falsely accused of paternity each year.

Any divorce attorney will tell you that courts are notorious for continuing child support even after it has been proved that the man named in the paternity case is not the real father. Imagine paying support for 18-21 years for a child who is *not yours*.

If 30% of all children are conceived by men other than those named by the mothers, then it's reasonable to consider that, with nearly 4 million children being born each year in the United States, up to 1.2 million men could be victims of paternity fraud annually.

The vast majority of these men are being enslaved by the courts and the mothers' lies. They are enslaved to support other men's children until at least age 18. Which means that millions of men are indentured either by marriage or the courts to pay a huge chunk of their income for children with whom they have no biological ties.

If 1.2 million men annually are victims of paternity fraud, then 12 million men may be enslaved by paternity fraud over a given 10-year period.

In 1861, nearly 4 million slaves were the catalysts for the Civil War – a war in which nearly a million men were killed or wounded. Out of that conflict came the Thirteenth Amendment to our Constitution: "Neither slavery nor involuntary servitude, except as a punishment for crime whereof the party shall have been duly convicted, shall exist within the United States, or any place subject to their jurisdiction."

Roughly 12% of men who refuse to pay child support do so because they are not the biological fathers, according to family court records. A man who refuses to pay support could be labeled a deadbeat dad under current law and practice, even when DNA evidence proves the child is not his. The law can take away his driver's license and other professional licenses and make it almost impossible for him to work, then throw him in jail for contempt of court – often without a hearing or jury trial.

Today in America, DNA evidence can free a convicted murderer from prison, but it *cannot free a man from child support payments or jail.*

More Than Equal

Women account for 83 cents of every dollar spent in America, yet earn only 38 cents of every dollar. They make up a large portion of the difference by spending their men's hard-earned money. And sadly for us, many women have come to consider this their birthright.

Helen Reddy's hit song of the 1970s was called, "I Am Woman, Hear Me Roar." It became an anthem for American women as they demanded and asserted their civil rights. Based on the outcome, it should have been called, "I Am Woman, See Me Spend."

American women are the most protected, wealthiest women on the planet, thanks in large part to the feminist ideologies that continue to exert influence over our government and courts. Hence, American women routinely demand that men shed their money, property, children, families and rights. They are disenfranchising men and stripping them of the very same rights that women have demanded and won.

This is not to say that women don't deserve equality. They do. Total equality. But the pendulum has swung too far in their favor and resulted in inequality for men.

Child Custody

On average, divorced dads spend about 80 days a year with their kids. That's less than 22% of the total days in a year, or roughly 1.5 days per week.

If that's acceptable to you, you'll do what about 90% of all dads do and concede custody to the mother. If you concede custody, then make sure you negotiate your visitation rights as part of your original agreement. This will save you thousands of dollars in legal fees you would otherwise spend obtaining standard visitation later.

There is a widely accepted notion in American society that children are always better off with their mothers. This theory is so widely accepted that most men believe it, too.

As with most feminist-instigated myths, the facts reveal a very different picture. Statistics taken from numerous marriage and family counseling surveys show the painful realities. Children raised without their fathers generally earn lower grades in school, suffer more emotional problems and get into more trouble with the law whether they are in or out of school.

Even worse, mothers are, generally speaking, far *more abusive* toward their children than are fathers. And mothers are far *less likely to pay* court-ordered child support to custodial and lower-earning fathers.

Unfortunately, these statistics and surveys don't get much play in the mass media because men are not prone to whining publicly about their problems. But women have a vested interest in maintaining the belief that they are the "weaker" sex, in need of financial, legal and social protection from men. They use their children to gain still more sympathy and greater protection under the law. The squeaky wheel gets the grease, especially in divorce-custody battles.

Some of the more startling facts about divorce-custody battles were revealed in *The Father's Emergency Guide to Divorce-Custody Battle: A Tour through the Predatory World of Judges, Lawyers, Psychologists and Social Workers in the Subculture of Divorce*, written in 1997 by divorce attorneys Robert Seidenberg, William Dawes and Lawrence Pekmezian. Based on their actual courtroom experience, they said:

"Custody litigation begins with a brief 'temporary' hearing at which custody, child support, alimony and possession of the marital home are 'temporarily' decided until a full trial can be held. In truth, what happens at this hearing is unlikely to change even if you spend $100,000 on a full trial.

"Women initiate the great majority of divorces. What's more, they start interviewing lawyers and planning their moves months before initiating action. A father typically doesn't have a clue to what's going on until he is served with a summons.

"A custody dispute typically begins with a legalized kidnapping. Since the goal is to establish one's self as the primary caretaker, lawyers advise women to take the children and leave; or to get a protective order evicting the husband from the house; or talk him into moving out 'for a trial separation.' Thus the mother can establish herself as the only caretaker, and secure sole custody at the temporary hearing. Most lawyers will not give this advice to men. But some do, and this strategy can work for men, too.

"The great majority of domestic violence and child sex abuse allegations made by women in custody litigation are false. They are made to gain advantage in custody, support and property determinations. Perjury is standard in domestic relations court. Lawyers know that perjury is the norm and many will advise their clients accordingly. They tend to do this with women far more than with men.

"Most lawyers have never won custody for a father. This is especially true of expensive lawyers reputed to be the best in the business.

"Many so-called custody disputes are not custody disputes at all. To avoid a costly court battle, many fathers concede custody right from the beginning, but then find they have to spend tens of thousands of dollars just to get 'standard' visitation.

"Child support is often exorbitant to the point of being financially crippling. It bears no relationship to the needs of the child, and for the average father it has the feeling of extortion. So-called 'deadbeat dads' are really 'refugee dads' who have been driven out of their children's lives by the courts, their ex-wives and bureaucracies."

In explaining how all this scandal could occur on a national basis without coming to public attention, Seidenberg, Dawes and Pekmezian enter the political realm. In a series of brief well-documented essays, they show how feminist ideology dominates public discourse to such a degree that few people even realize there is another side to these issues.

Too many American women have also bought into the feminist myth that females can have it all – fulfilling careers, devoted husbands and loving families. The truth is, they can't.

Like Superman, Superwoman only exists in the minds of movie and TV writers. In reality, very few people have it all. If you give 100% to your career, what's left for your spouse and family? It's not a male or female issue. It's a human issue.

Lose Your Spouse and Keep Your House

"No one can make you feel inferior without your consent."
– Anna Eleanor Roosevelt, 1884-1962

The majority of divorced men lose their homes to ex-wives. Some have the resources to move out and maintain separate residences. Some have so little money left after alimony and child support they end up living with friends, in their cars or even homeless.

But you can keep your house even if you don't have the financial resources for a prolonged legal battle. So how exactly do you lose your spouse and keep your house?

First, a little back story…

Shortly after I told my ex I wanted the divorce, she consulted a high-powered, high-priced attorney who, according to her, had never lost a case. She said he wanted $10,000 for the pleasure of taking her on as a client and taking me to the cleaners. Knowing what a greedy woman I was dealing with, I responded that paying $10,000 to an attorney would mean *$10,000 less for her.*

She agreed to keep the money for herself rather quickly, as I suspected. After 19 years with her, I knew that her primary motivation was greed. This is fairly common among American women. Faced with the same choice, most women will choose the money for themselves. Keep that in mind when you start your negotiations.

Your objective is to keep your negotiations between you and your spouse, with as little outside influence as possible. Avoid attorneys at all costs. It is advisable to consult one on your own, but only one who offers a free initial consultation. You mainly want to take advantage of the free consultation to learn more about your legal rights. Most attorneys offer free consults because it gives them an opportunity to assess your case and assess you as a potential client.

Here's a real-life example.

Let's say you are married without children. You own a condominium and few, if any, other assets. You owe $20,000 in combined credit card debt and $10,000 on a personal loan. You've made all the payments on your home and you want to keep it.

Do not, under any circumstances, move out.

Let your spouse know that you plan to stay and keep the condo, no matter what. If you have a home office or run a business from home, let her know how important it is that your address remain the same. If you don't run a business from your home, find other reasons why you must stay and why it will benefit her to leave.

Make it uncomfortable for her to be in the home.

Declare your refusal to move. If you are adamant about it, there's a good chance she'll eventually leave by default. Maybe condo living is less than ideal for her. Maybe bad memories are enough to send her packing. Maybe she hates a certain after-shave you use or music you play or that you never put the toilet seat down. Use that after-shave. Play that music. And never ever put the seat down.

Maybe she has already made other living arrangements. Maybe she needs some extra money to start her new life.

Make it clear that she will be compensated for leaving. If you live in a community property state, she has legal right to half your home. If you stay, you will have to buy out her share.

In effect, you are paying her to leave. This will likely appeal to her greed, too.

Let's say you purchased the condo for $140,000. It is now worth $180,000. Selling the condo would net about $40,000 in gross profit. After real estate commissions and closing fees, you would net $30,000. Her share of that would be $15,000. Since you want to keep the condo, you will have to pay her $15,000 to buy out her interest, as if you were selling it at the current market price.

Make sure she signs a quitclaim deed in exchange for the cash.

You don't want her name to remain on your property's title or deed, and you don't want her to have any legal claims to the property.

That's the purpose of a quitclaim deed. It's a legal document that allows her to sign over all rights to the property. The quitclaim deed also protects her from tax liabilities or any liens you may incur on the property after she's gone. Make sure she understands these benefits. If you are Internet-savvy, you can find sample quitclaim deeds online and download them to your hard drive. You can also find samples at your local library, office supplies store or bookstore. Legal form services can also provide you with blank quitclaim deeds.

Let's say your spouse also has $20,000 in credit card debt. Your legal share in most community property states, even if you haven't spent a dime of that money yourself, is $10,000. Add that to the $15,000 representing her share of the profit on the condo for a total of $25,000. Remember to subtract her half of any personal loans you acquired while married. This will reduce the total amount you owe her.

At this point, she may be feeling that you want her out so badly, you'd be willing to pay more. She might also be adding to your tab as compensation for her pain and suffering, especially if you instigated the divorce (which you should). She might demand a lump sum of $30,000 or more for the pleasure of losing her company.

Resist the temptation to give her what she wants. Negotiate for the actual amount you owe her. Remind her of your own pain and suffering. After all, it's not easy to instigate divorce, either. And you may be feeling guilt about divorcing her. Which is probably a big part of why so few men do it.

If that doesn't work, counter her proposal with $20,000. Look at the rest of her terms and see if anything else can be negotiated in your favor. Remember that the legal owner of the residence will gain tax advantages for the long term, but also have to pay for home maintenance and repairs, which can be costly.

In my case, these head-to-head negotiations went on for eight days. She kept agreeing to my terms, then reversing herself a day later, after consulting with her "friends." That's why you should eliminate as many outside influences as possible during your negotiations.

Some of her friends may be absolute bitches, just itching for the chance to make some "male" suffer. And some of those friends may be attorneys, divorce financial planners or accountants. Regardless, you can be sure of one thing: They are not *your* friends. And the advice they give her will cost you more money in the end.

Once you've finished your negotiations with her, type up your agreement and have her sign it. Make it as specific as possible, especially regarding property divisions and time frames. If you don't feel comfortable doing this on your own, find some divorce agreements and financial disclosure forms or worksheets on the Internet, at your local library or bookstore or your nearest family courthouse. After you've completed the forms, type them up, have her sign them and take them to a local legal service (find them in the Yellow Pages or online) for all the necessary court filings. Remember to have her sign the quitclaim deed, too.

Make sure the agreement and quitclaim deed are filed with the court.

Confirm that the legal service has filed all the necessary paperwork with the court. I didn't and almost paid for it with my home. My ex and I had signed the divorce agreement and the quitclaim deed and turned them over to a legal service. I assumed they would file all the papers with the court. A few weeks later, my ex moved across the country. I mailed her a cashier's check for her lump sum settlement two weeks after that. End of story, right?

Flash forward eight months.

Interest rates had dropped substantially, so I decided to refinance. There was enough equity to combine my first mortgage and the second mortgage (used to fund her lump-sum payment) into one payment. With interest rates so low, the new payment would be equal to the old payment, even with the second mortgage added in.

Successful refinancing would mean goodbye second mortgage. Goodbye all unpaid balances related to the divorce. I would have a new lease on life.

There was just one hitch in the plan. My ex's name was still on the title. The refinancing company wanted her to sign a new quitclaim deed before approving the transaction. They claimed that no prior quitclaim deed was filed. Of course, she refused to sign another one, so they denied my application citing that I did not have clear title.

The whole deal fell apart.

I took several weeks to regroup. During that time, I received a letter from an attorney stating that his client (my ex!), though already remarried and living across the country with her new family, wanted to reopen the case. She claimed that she still had legal right to the condo (she was still on the title) and that she had signed the divorce agreement under duress and the influence of prescription drugs.

She also claimed I withheld my true assets from her. So her attorney required me to legally disclose my finances to the court – something we had not done when we filed our original agreement. She wanted to take my condo, even though I had already bought out her interest and compensated her with a lump-sum payment.

I might have given up at this point (many men do), hired an attorney of my own and fought a prolonged, expensive legal battle to keep my home. But I didn't.

Instead, I decided to represent myself and fight. I made things as difficult for her and her attorney as possible. If I could drag the proceedings on long enough, her money (actually her new husband's money) would eventually run out. I also knew that she had already signed a quitclaim deed and that it was legally binding. I just had to figure out why it was never filed, find it and get it filed before she could take the condo away.

If you find yourself in this position, ask her attorney for extensions on everything to buy time. It's your legal right. Insist on at least a 90-day extension for your financial disclosures. You can cite the pressures of full-time employment or outside business responsibilities. You will need to reconstruct your exact financial picture at the time your divorce agreement was signed, which will take time. Her attorney will agree.

Ask her attorney for his or her "bar number," too. The American Bar Association assigns a license number to every attorney. If you are representing yourself, you have a right to this information. Later, if you have a complaint about her attorney, his/her bar number will come in handy. It's also a subtle way of telling her attorney you mean business.

Use the extra time to complete the lengthy financial disclosure. If you've never handled the finances before, get help from a trusted male friend (in matters of divorce, a male friend will likely be more willing to help you). Call the legal service firm to determine what happened to your original quitclaim deed, which should have been filed along with the original divorce agreement.

Call your mortgage company, explain your situation and ask for advice. They might tell you, as mine did, that the original quitclaim deed was never filed. All I had to do was find the original and they would file it properly. A new title would then be created in my name.

Make copies of everything related to your divorce and keep them in a safe place. You may need to refer to them later or show proof of your claims. If you need help getting organized, buy one of those tabbed file organizers from an office supplies store and set it up so it's easy for you to find what you need when you need it.

While I kept her and her attorney busy with extensions, demands and counterclaims, I found the original quitclaim deed with her signature and called my bank. They told me to make a copy for my records and overnight them the original.

Within a week, the quitclaim deed was properly filed. The $155 filing fee was added to the new refinance deal with my mortgage company. Refinancing forced the change in title and wiped out the balance of my divorce debt.

It took nearly eight months to fight off the ex and her attorney. During that time, I kept him very busy, answering registered letters and a flurry of emails while I quietly resolved the quitclaim deed problem and refinanced the condo out from under her.

I was home free. The second mortgage was rolled into the first. The new payment was within a few dollars of the original. And she and her attorney evaporated into thin air. I'm not sure why, though I suspect it was because she had stopped paying him. And the new title was in my name only.

Your situation may be similar or entirely different. The key, regardless of your situation, is to stay in the house no matter what, make her as uncomfortable as you possibly can *without doing anything violent or illegal*, negotiate your settlement without attorneys and make sure all the necessary paperwork is filed with the court.

If you cannot, for whatever reason, lose your spouse and keep your house, consider another alternative most people are unaware of. It's a legal concept called *"nesting."* This is where the children remain in the home and the parents rotate in and out much like birds tending a nest. This often works to the children's advantage in joint custody agreements by giving them home stability. But it can be a huge inconvenience for parents who must make alternative living arrangements for that part of the week they are not in the children's home.

You Can Fight the Law and Win!

*"It is better to be a mouse in a cat's mouth
than a man in a lawyer's hands."*
– Spanish proverb

Attorneys are adversarial by nature and profession. They get paid to argue. They are also very expensive, charging you anywhere from $150 to $400 per hour to "represent" you in your divorce proceedings. While your attorney argues with her attorney, both of their billing meters keep running. Then there are court costs and filing fees on top of that.

So how do you avoid the obscenely high cost of attorneys?

Don't hire attorneys!

It will be easier, less costly and much quicker to negotiate with your soon-to-be ex. If there's so much anger and acrimony between you and your ex that you cannot arrive at an acceptable settlement within a couple of weeks, seek mediation or arbitration.

Divorce mediators can be found in the Yellow Pages or on the Internet. It'll still be cheaper than hiring attorneys, and you'll often get through the proceedings quicker and with fewer headaches.

In addition to saving you thousands of dollars on your settlement, they'll help you keep more of your hard-earned money. One couple I know saved over $30,000 in legal fees by doing a *pro se* divorce. Another couple spent over $100,000 on lawyers and legal fees to obtain a traditional divorce because they could not reach an agreement by themselves.

Divorce lawyers can be quite despicable. They have a knack for turning even the most amicable couples against each other, especially when it comes to children, child support and property settlements.

Your future ex is likely a far less formidable opponent *without* an attorney. And your divorce will likely cost far less if you work it out between yourselves – like the mature adults you are supposed to be.

PART THREE:

Surviving After Divorce

*"It is seldom indeed that one parts
on good terms, because if one were
on good terms one would not part."*

– Marcel Proust, 1871-1922

Friends and Lovers

According to *Men's Health* magazine, about half of all divorced men remain friends with their ex-wives. One in five even continue to have sex with their ex-wives.

If you can remain friends, with or without sex, more power to you. Building and maintaining a healthy friendship with your ex is far more important when children are involved. Your children need you to be friends. They need to experience peace and love and mutual respect in their lives from their adult role models. They don't need you bickering or belittling each other like you did when you were together. Children tend to take those behaviors personally, often blaming themselves for their parents' failures.

Now, more than ever, your children need positive role models. This is your opportunity to set a good example for them on what relationships can and should be like.

Accept that the marriage is over and that it's not all your fault.

Some men cannot accept that their marriage has failed and never move on. Instead, they are so devastated that they remain locked in a state of quiet depression and loneliness for years and often for the remainder of their lives.

More often than not, men blame themselves for the divorce. Their self-esteem plummets. They stop taking care of themselves and fall into unhealthy behaviors such as drinking and drug abuse. They are twice as likely as women to commit suicide immediately after a divorce.

If the average man first experiences divorce at about age 30 and lives to be about 75, what does he do for the next 45 years? You can waste 45 years being depressed and angry or invest it in discovering the best that life has to offer.

Manage your anger constructively.

If you're angry, find a constructive way to get it off your chest. Take up martial arts or running or join a gym. Spend 20 to 30 minutes blasting away at a heavy bag or some other physical activity that helps you blow off steam. Throw yourself into a home-remodeling project. Demolishing your old kitchen cabinets, for example, can be an excellent way to vent your anger and aggression.

Deal with your feelings openly and constructively.

It's easy to slip into denial or depression over divorce. But keeping your emotions bottled up inside can place enormous stress on your body. It can literally make you sick.

If you are depressed, find someone to talk to. There's no shame in seeing a psychologist or counselor to help you explore your feelings and get past them.

You and your ex may still love and care for each other as people, even after you realize you cannot live together under the same roof. If there are no children involved, decide whether friendship with your ex is important or beneficial to you. If so, pursue it at your own risk. Because it is highly unlikely that you will recapture the same romantically charged feelings you had when you first got married.

Sleep with your ex at your own risk.

It may sound crazy, but 20% of divorced men continue having sex with their ex-wives. Aside from the familiarity and convenience, these liaisons generally do little to help you get past the divorce. They may even set you back on your road to recovery.

Instead, look for new activities to enjoy. You might discover new friends to enjoy those activities with, too. If you take part in an activity you enjoy with like-minded people, you may start a new friendship with at least one common interest.

Create new rituals and start new traditions that are uniquely yours. This is your time to live the kind of life you can love.

You may have to leave some old friends behind in your quest for a new, improved life. If you are like most men, you and your ex probably had married friends; other couples you shared various activities with. If you maintain a relationship with your ex, you may also choose to maintain friendships with your circle of married couples.

But if you and your ex part bitterly, you may have to accept that your married friends will now have to chose whether they will remain friends with you or your ex. One or both of you may move away from the neighborhood, making it difficult or impossible to maintain those friendships.

This is the perfect time to make a fresh start. *When one door closes, another opens.*

As you reenter "bachelorhood," your true friends will make themselves known to you. True friends never get in your way and always stand by you. True friends give you support and encouragement.

Learn from your past mistakes and start making better choices for yourself today.

What if you find someone who is more than a friend or lover? What if you find someone you think you want to be with; someone you can be yourself with; someone who respects you and gives you the space you need?

If you find someone like that, great! The best relationships are the ones that afford both partners plenty of space to be themselves. If it feels right to you, do it.

If you don't want another relationship and prefer to remain

a free man, that's great, too, as long as it's your choice. There are many advantages to living solo. Like doing whatever you want, whenever you want. Like not having to interact with another person every day and every night. Like not compromising your lifestyle.

Are You Ready for Freedom?

"To cheat one's self out of love is the greatest deception
of which there is no reparation in either time or eternity."
– Soren Kierkegaard, 1813-1855

After being off the market through a decade or two of marriage, discovering your freedom and jumping back into the dating scene can be a daunting experience. A whole generation may have passed and brought in the age of computers and the Internet. That's why most men choose to wait three to six months before dating again. They need time to regroup and acclimate to their new surroundings.

Are you ready for freedom? Are you ready for a new relationship? If not, how will you know when you are?

Ten Reasons Why You May Not be Ready for Another Woman

If any of the following statements applies to you, consider staying unattached for a while longer. You're probably not ready for a relationship quite yet.

1. You blame women for most of the problems in your life.
2. You still have overpowering feelings of anger directed toward women.
3. You describe your dating prospects only in terms of their looks.
4. You feel contempt for people who are in love.
5. You seek out only married women or other poor dating prospects.
6. You are extremely critical of others.
7. You have unrealistic expectations of your dating prospects.
8. You're unwilling to compromise.
9. You're abusing alcohol or drugs.
10. You believe that all women are like your ex.

If none of those statements applies to you, you are emotionally healthy enough to begin dating again. If you are ready for the next step, there are many new options.

Seven Ways to Earn Back Your Self-Respect

If married life has eroded your self-respect, you need to rebuild it. Here are seven ways you can do just that:

1. **Get a better job:** If you've been in a rut, maybe it's time to polish up your resume and image and start looking for a new job, a better-paying job or even a new career. Often, ex-wives exert an undeniable influence over our jobs. Maybe she didn't like you traveling or working long hours. Maybe you caved in to her wishes and took a job that wasn't as fulfilling, challenging or enjoyable for you. Now you can pursue what you want.

2. **Upgrade yourself:** Take a training course or go back to school. Take up a new hobby or do something else you've always wanted to do. The effort and the lessons you learn from it will help you rebuild your self-confidence.

3. **Spend time with friends:** Get out of the house. Have some laughs. Do something you might not have done on your own in the past.

4. **Flush away the negatives:** Eliminate bad memories by trashing, shredding or burning them. Eliminate bitterness by talking through your feelings with a trusted friend or counselor and taking up activities that give you pleasure.

5. **Forgive yourself:** Millions of men fail at marriage. The failure was not entirely your fault. Forgive the part that was.

6. **Defy the odds:** Just because your divorced friends are miserable, it doesn't mean you have to be miserable.
No matter how tough life is, rise above it. You can improve every facet of your life through the force of sheer will. Remember you're making your own life decisions now, not someone elses'.

7. Date when you're ready: Once the scars have healed and you're feeling good about yourself again, go out and meet some new women!

How to Meet Women

The Internet has given us fast, cheap access to millions of women worldwide. We can now do what we used to do in bars… online. Today, men are meeting, dating, hooking up, playing the field, building relationships and even marrying women they meet online.

If you feel like you've been dropped in the middle of a brave new world, you're not alone. Today, strangers approach each another via email or in virtual online chat rooms before graduating to cell phone calls and meetings at Starbucks to decide whether to venture out on a first date or have a one-night stand.

Except for computers and the Internet, most of these resources didn't exist in 1980. Now, email, online chat rooms, cell phones and Starbucks are ubiquitous. For computer-literate men, it means more options and greater opportunities to meet more women quickly and inexpensively.

You can wait several months before you start dating or throw yourself back into the social scene with a vengeance. If your ego has been damaged from marriage and divorce, you may consider dating right away to help regain your confidence. If you think striking out with a woman will kill your ego, hold off on dating until you're strong enough to handle a few let-downs. It might help to remind yourself that all guys strike out from time to time.

If you are still in your 20s, you'll have better chances with the 30-something divorcees who may be looking for a no-strings affair with a younger, more energetic man. If you are in your 30s, the 20-something females are fair game for an older guy who is more established. If you are in your 40s or 50s, the field can be wide open or very narrow, depending on how much money (and energy) you have. Keep in mind that most women tend to find wealthy men very attractive no matter what they look like.

If you have female friends, they may want to procure dates for you. This rarely works out to your benefit. Letting a female friend choose your dating prospects is like letting your mom choose your clothes. If you don't like blind dates and want more control, try a dating service or an Internet dating site.

If you prefer meeting women in person, try bars, pubs or clubs. Invest some time researching the types of women who frequent those places. Notice how they dress and how the other guys dress, too. You don't necessarily have to blend in, but you don't want to stand out like a sore thumb, either. Suits don't fit with a blue-jeans crowd (though you might capture the attention of *every woman* in the place). And if you're old enough to own a leisure suit, burn it. It won't work anywhere.

Try wearing all black to give yourself a dark, mysterious, edgy look.

How you carry yourself and conduct yourself is as important as how you look. Many newly single men appear nervous at first, or lonely, or desperate. If you eyeball every woman in the club like a fresh piece of meat, they will sense your motives (you're up to no good) and avoid you like a social disease.

The best way to interest a woman is to ignore her.

 Most women are attention whores. They expect you to look at them. Don't.

Instead, enjoy your beer and act as if you own the place. Do this quietly, as if you don't want people to know you own the place. If you can come across as only interested in having a couple of drinks and too cool for the room, women will frequently be drawn to you. To attract their attention, deny them yours.

Don't expect this to work halfway into your first drink. It may take an hour or two before a woman approaches you. But one or more women will approach. And it's a safe bet that any woman who approaches you has already decided she finds you attractive.

Best of all, you haven't spent a dime on her.

When you see the handwriting on the wall, pay attention.

As the saying goes, "If you keep doing what you're doing, you'll keep getting what you're getting." Do you still want what you got from your ex all those years?

Ask yourself the important questions. Who am I? What do I want? Why do I want it? Through dating, you can often learn just as much about the qualities you don't want in a partner as the qualities you do want. That is, if you want a partner at all.

It is better to be alone than wish you were.

If you can't find the right woman, don't be afraid to go solo. There's a huge difference between living free and living in hell. You can date as many women as you want and do as much or as little you please. There are far worse ways for a man to live. They usually involve prison or marriage.

Don't live with a woman unless you plan to marry her.

Regular sex is *not* a good reason for you to live with someone. You can live apart and still have sex as often as you want. And you don't have to live with a woman because you think she's the only one who will have you. There are about 145 million women in America and hundreds of millions more in Canada and overseas. Despite what your ex may have told you, do you really think that she's the only one out of billions who will have you?

How to Translate Femalese

If you've met someone you like and started dating again, congratulations! You will now be called upon to use the communication skills you learned while you were married. In case marriage didn't teach you basic communication skills, here's a quick refresher course to help you understand what a woman really means when she speaks.

1. "Yes" means no.
2. "No" means yes.
3. "Maybe" means no.
4. "We need" means she wants.
5. "I'm sorry" means you'll be sorry.
6. "We need to talk" means she needs to complain.
7. "Sure, go ahead" means she'd rather you didn't.
8. "Do what you want" means you'll pay for it later.
9. "I'm not upset" means of course she's upset, you moron!
10. "Are you listening to me?" means she's not done complaining.
11. "Communicate with me" means agree with her.
12. "Turn out the lights" means she wants to pretend you're someone else.
13. "Turn out the lights" means she can't stand the sight of your beer belly.
14. "Turn out the lights" means don't look at anything that might turn you on.
15. "You're so manly" means you need a shave and/or you sweat like a pig.
16. "Do you love me?" means she's about to ask for something expensive.
17. "It's your decision" means it's never your decision.

18. "Isn't there a game on tonight?" means is sex all you ever think about?
19. "I'll be ready in a minute" means find a game to watch, preferably a double-header.
20. "How much do you love me?" means she just spent the last dime of your savings.

The little refresher course above is intended for jest, but only barely.

Remember that women communicate very differently than men. They communicate with subtle cues, often indirectly, and assume you will understand. They often communicate just for the sake of communication, without any specific goal in mind. Men are typically more direct, more goal-oriented and more focused on outcomes or results.

The Ultimate Extreme Makeover

"Living well is the best revenge."
– George Herbert, 1593-1633

One of the best things you can do for yourself after a divorce is the ultimate extreme makeover. You can also call it cleansing, exorcism or rebirth. No matter what you call it, the end result should be a better quality of life for you. So, where do you begin?

1. Start with a blank sheet of paper.
2. Draw a line down the center.
3. On the left side list all the things you like about your life.
4. On the right side list all the things you don't like.

Include as many items as you can think of – everything from where you live to where you work and what you do for a living. Include your friends, social activities, clothes, appearance, hobbies, possessions and personal habits. Include anything and everything you can think of. Nothing is too small for this list. When you're done, you'll have the beginning of an outline on how to live the perfect life for *you*.

But making a list is just the first step. Once your list is complete, prioritize everything according to its importance to you. Ask yourself what you'd most like to change about your life.

Be fearless. Take on the big issues first. If your job is a major source of dissatisfaction and stress, start there. Think about the steps you must take in order to make a job change. Polish up your resume. Talk to trusted friends and associates. Organize your contact list. Figure out just what it is that you really want to do.

Plan all of the steps necessary for change. Then take action. Remember this is about doing something to make your life better. It's not about idle dreaming or wishful thinking.

Your Home is Your Castle

If moving is not an option right now, consider remodeling your living space, whether it's a house, a condo or an apartment. After all, the place is now yours to arrange as you please, so why not arrange it to *your* liking?

Start by getting rid of everything you don't want in your living space. If it has lace, frills or flowers on it, you probably don't want it. It probably reminds you of her.

Donate anything in decent condition to a local charity or recycling center. Some charities and recycling centers will even come to your home and haul heavy items away for you. Best of all, you get to write off charitable donations on your income taxes (if you itemize deductions). Calculate the value of anything you give to charity based on fair market prices. In other words, if you give away used furniture, don't deduct the cost of new furniture.

Trash or give away anything else you don't want or need. Reclaim your space so you have room to surround yourself with things you enjoy, even if what you enjoy most is simply more space. If you're happy with nothing more than a cool recliner and a big-screen TV, then that's all you should have. Just don't go out and buy it with money you don't have.

Most men fight to keep their homes, their cars, their dogs and their big-screen TVs – and little else – when they divorce. Most men are minimalists – they don't like having too much "stuff" around.

Despite what your ex may have told you, there's nothing wrong with being a minimalist. Minimalists believe that less is more. Minimalists can move from place to place more easily because they don't accumulate things the way most people do. Minimalists rarely have to do spring cleaning.

Reduce Your Costs and Increase Your Satisfaction

The financial toll taken by divorce and paying off debts can be harsh. If you can't afford to have your space remodeled, consider doing most of the work yourself.

There are numerous do-it-yourself home remodeling books, magazines, websites and an entire TV network (*DIY*) that show you, step-by-step, how to do virtually everything, including carpentry, electrical and plumbing projects. You'll gain useful knowledge and skills while saving anywhere from 50% to 90% (cost of labor) on each project you complete yourself.

If you decide to take this route, watch every home improvement and do-it-yourself show on TV and borrow or buy books on home improvement and repair. Home Depot has a great collection of home improvement books and magazines that cover everything you need to know. They also offer free live demonstrations and workshops about all kinds of do-it-yourself projects. Other home centers have similar offerings.

Even if you don't consider yourself "handy," give it a try. It beats paying other guys to do the work for you. It also helps you spend your money more wisely – a huge plus if divorce and its aftermath set you back financially. And it will give you something constructive to do while you're getting over your divorce.

Ultimately, the satisfaction you gain from doing it yourself is priceless. And it may even add to the value of your home.

Remodel Your Social Life

If you had become a stay-at-home couch potato while you were married, get out and enjoy as much of the outside world as possible now. Even if you have to push yourself out the door to break out of your rut, do it. Spend more time with your friends. Go to movies, sports events, concerts, art exhibits, parties, pool halls, museums (there are all kinds of museums) or strip clubs – whatever interests you.

If you never traveled much when you were with your ex, now is your chance to make up for lost time. In almost 20 years with my ex, I traveled very little. But in just the first two years after she left, I trekked to England, Scotland, the Netherlands, France, Belgium, Mexico, Hawaii, North Carolina and up and down the coast of California. Fortunately, I only paid for two of these trips myself.

As with any remodeling project, there are financial responsibilities that come with the territory. Don't spend more than you can afford on anything. Charging a trip around the world to your credit cards is probably not the most responsible idea.

Try something new. Make new friends. If your ex-wife made you feel unattractive while you were married, then rebuild your self-confidence one date at a time. Don't let fear hold you back. You have a new social life ahead of you. And every minute you spend feeling sad, depressed or lonely is another minute of your life lost forever.

Avoid falling into relationships that are similar to your marriage.

For many men who resist change, even a miserable relationship can become as comfortable as an old shoe. Even if it has holes, lacks support and causes you pain, it's still well broken in. If you find yourself falling into this comfort zone in your relationships, break out before it's too late.

Recognize behavior patterns that may be reminiscent of your marriage and break away from them. Figure out what you *really* want. After all, why would you want to repeat the same mistake and suffer again?

Sport Dating

What if you are not looking for love? What if finding another committed relationship is out of the question for you? What if you want to make up for lost time and play the field? And what if you just want to add a slew of new notches to your bedpost?

You're not alone. Most singles say they are looking for "companionship," not marriage. You can, too. You can get back in the social swing and meet a variety of very interesting and very different women. You can add to your life experiences.

Meeting and dating lots of different women can be fun. The variety suits most men while they learn more about what they really want and don't want.

The Internet offers a low-cost, efficient way to approach sport dating. Your online experiences are like hunting expeditions. You can meet hundreds of women online almost every night. Their Internet profiles are often more revealing than a few ordinary dates or bar pick-ups, and the whole process is considerably more compressed.

You can meet a woman online, exchange a few emails and phone numbers and, next thing you know, she's at your place removing her clothes – all in a span of a few days.

The Internet is an excellent place to conduct your search, especially if you are between 30 and 50 years old. It is the fastest, cheapest, most effective way to meet women today. But it can be one of the most frustrating experiences of your life if you take a haphazard approach to it. It can also be less time-consuming (you can avoid spending hundreds of hours online looking for Ms. Right or Ms. Right Now) and less expensive (you can avoid paying for all those dinner, movie and concert dates).

To avoid all that time, pain and expense, read *The Ultimate Man's Guide™ to Internet Dating*. If you are not looking for a serious relationship or friendship and just want a sex partner, focus on adult-oriented sites such as Alt.com or AdultFriendFinder.com. There you will find 25 million members worldwide and lots of women who want exactly what you want, from a no-strings sexual liaison to a meaningful relationship.

Looking for Love Again

If you are looking for love again, it is possible to find someone you are compatible with – someone who fits your core criteria – online. Core criteria are those qualities you absolutely must have in a partner – or those you consider deal-breakers. Core criteria might include such things as honesty, financial independence, religious beliefs, race, intelligence or a way of looking at life. Physical qualities that change over time are not core criteria.

Be flexible.

You may be reluctant to date single moms but open to the possibility. If you are looking for women aged 25 to 35, for example, you'll find that a majority of women in that range are single moms with young children or preteens. In pure marketing terms, eliminating single moms from consideration could reduce your pool of potential dates by half. The real issue is whether or not having children in your life is one of your core criteria.

Recognize how you have grown and changed over time.

As you age, you also change in ways both obvious and subtle. Maybe you didn't want kids while in your 20s or 30s because you were too busy establishing your career.

Ten or 20 years later, you may realize that raising a child is not just about the responsibilities and sacrifices, it's also about the joy and personal gratification of helping mold a child into a good human being, while opening yourself up to unconditional love.

Ultimately, it's about making yourself happy. But you have to know who you really are and what you really want before you can achieve happiness. You have to know your likes and dislikes, your wants and needs, first.

Finding a woman who meets your criteria won't necessarily be easy. But if that's what you want, in the end, it will be worth every effort you give.

You can invest time and money generously in your life-remodeling project or do it frugally. You can do more or less, depending on what you really want and what you're willing to do to get what you want. The choices are all yours.

Seven Steps to Living the Life You Always Wanted.

1. Let it out. If you don't let your emotions out, they'll eat away at you, and so will your ex's memory. Let yourself have one last good cry or temper tantrum. Then let it go.

2. Retrain yourself. You will forget your ex once you can see her in a true light. Use creative visualization to imagine what you want. Close your eyes and picture negative images, like the time she criticized you in front of your family or friends. In your mind, build an impenetrable wall between yourself and those experiences. Use your imagination to forever banish those energy-draining, poisonous emotions.

3. Do a profit-and-loss statement. The end of marriage is a great time to learn more about yourself and your ability to function as a married or single individual. List the pluses and the minuses of your marriage. Analyze what was right and wrong about your old relationship and your role in it. Be honest with yourself. The success of your future relationships depends on it. You may discover that you gained as much as you lost. If nothing else, you will learn to forge better relationships in the future.

4. Start a "guys night out" club. Weekends can be tough for a newly single guy. Call your friends early in the week to make plans for a Friday or Saturday night. Have a standing Friday night poker game or go to sporting events, parties or concerts with your buddies.

5. Reject rebounds. Rebounds are great when your favorite basketball team is making them. But they're bad when you're talking about new relationships. If you find yourself falling back "in love" soon after your divorce, look at the new woman for who she really is, not as a cure for your loneliness. You can't cure loneliness simply by replacing the love object. You've got to get over your ex completely before you can really move on.

6. Lock the door and throw away the key. Let it be over. If she keeps calling to say that she wants to stay friends with you (or some other pretext), don't fall for it. Cut her loose for good and celebrate the new, improved, I won't-settle-for-anything-less you.

7. Discover an awesome new man: yourself. Do all the things you've been dying to try or that you'd put on hold because she disapproved. Enroll in a class, research a new career, throw yourself into a home improvement project, take a trip or take up a new hobby as long as your finances can handle it.

American Woman, Stay Away From Me

"A variety of nothing is superior to a monotony of something."
– Johann Paul Friedrich Richter, 1763-1825

If you are in post-divorce dating mode and you've been out of circulation for a long time, you may have some sense that American women have changed since the last time you were single. They have. And they have manipulated the majority of the country into changing along with them.

Whether you are contemplating dating again or already in the thick of it, you need to understand how traditional male and female roles have changed in American society. If nothing else, it will give you a different perspective on the new "battle of the sexes."

In a nutshell, women now "wear the pants" in America. Whether you realize it or not, female influences are all around you. They have incredible power over home life, the entertainment industry and even the workplace. Women today make most of the household decisions about virtually everything from healthcare to home decorating. They control a large portion of what we watch on television. They've infused the workplace with a flurry of new rules, codes, sexual harassment guidelines and a greater focus on processes than results. They hold sway over government and divorce courts. They've even invaded the last bastions of American manhood, the locker rooms of male professional athletes and sports pages of your local newspaper.

I interviewed hundreds of men aged 25 to 55 during the research for this book. They echoed the same sentiments over and over. Men are simply fed up with the changing attitudes of American women and the systematic emasculation of

American males that's been in progress and gaining strength for over 25 years.

How many times have you heard the cliché that "men don't stop and ask for directions"? Women say it so often, even some *men* believe it. But is it true? Isn't it also true that most men have an excellent sense of direction, the ability to read and understand maps and that's often why we don't stop and ask for directions? But, more importantly, we're socialized to solve problems on our own without seeking the advice of others.

So much "fun" is poked at American men today that hardly anyone notices it. America has become a nation of women, by women and for women.

Today, little boys are suspended from grade school for playing cowboys and Indians or cops and robbers or any other variation of "good guy vs. bad guy" that helps them learn the difference between right and wrong. In one instance, a *4-year-old* was threatened with suspension for bringing a plastic Power Ranger action figure to his *day-care center*. The reason given: Action toys encourage rough play among little boys.

Isn't "rough play" a natural inclination among little boys? Isn't it a normal part of little boys' development into men? Isn't that how we've always been socialized in American society?

It was until the feminist movement changed everything. Today, our sons are given Ritalin so their natural aggressiveness, curiosity and restlessness can be chemically controlled, instead of nurtured and directed. How did we get here, anyway?

America has become first and foremost, a culture that is dominated by mommies. It wasn't always so: There was a time when fathers made most of the household decisions, went to work and tinkered with their cars while mothers stayed home, nested with the children and kept the family well-fed and satisfied.

But as the 20th century evolved, women's roles in society changed and they got more involved in politics, industry and the media. Many stopped cooking and cleaning and nurturing, proclaimed their freedom of choice and embarked on careers outside the home. Government became more intrusive and protective. The feminine influence on politics emphasized *social security* over national security. Their influence on divorce litigation and child custody laws emphasized the needs of women and children over the needs of men.

Male-Bashing in the Media Affects Divorce, Too

"If you've got a mother, a sister, a girlfriend,
a wife or a daughter, you are being trained."
– Jeff Foxworthy

Since the feminist revolution, there has been a concerted effort to denigrate men, reduce them to buffoons and render them weak and impotent, figuratively speaking. If you doubt this, then take a closer look at TV, because TV is a reliable barometer of American culture, particularly our steady diet of sitcoms and commercials.

In the 1950s, TV dads began to be portrayed as lovable goofballs (e.g. Dick Van Dyke) – perhaps the beginning of the trend. Yet, even in the 1950s, Dad was still the one who brought home the bacon and provided the main source of discipline (*Father Knows Best*).

Remember the classic TV line: "Wait 'til your father gets home." This was turned upside down in the 1970s with a prime-time cartoon of the same name.

From that, we created new shows that further epitomize the feminization of men.

Tim Allen's great comedy routine about being a man's man was reduced to a dumb sitcom called *Home Improvement*. It should have been called *Male Improvement*, because that's what every single episode was about. Tim's shrewish TV wife spent most of her time turning Tim into a "better" person, instead of just leaving him alone to be himself and restore that classic car in his garage.

Everyone Loves Raymond is another popular sitcom that persistently pokes fun at its male characters. It seems everyone loves poor goofy Raymond except for his bossy, controlling wife, who belittles and ridicules him in every episode, then punishes him by withholding sexual favors when he misbehaves (i.e., acts like a man). Ironically, about the only manly pursuit Ray gets to really enjoy is his job as a sports writer.

Finally, there's the TV show that epitomizes what American society has become: *Queer Eye for the Straight Guy*. Five gay males tell straight males how to dress and decorate, and the show has taken the popular culture by storm.

Judging by the ratings, many people find *Queer Eye* entertaining. But the implication of the show – where a bunch of homosexuals try to "make over" heterosexual guys into something "better" (i.e., more acceptable to women) by changing their clothes, home décor and music – is that "normal" men aren't good enough. Women, of course, love this show. Three out of four *Queer Eye* viewers are female.

Capitalizing on Queer Eye's success, Turner Broadcasting has jumped into the fray with the latest TV travesty against men. It's called "He's a Lady." This show starts with 11 men and makes them over into women. A panel of judges rates their beauty. Not surprisingly, only women find this funny. After all, they're the ones who will buy the products advertised during the commercial breaks.

From the male perspective, the show is insulting and demeaning. The implicit message is that we are not good enough, unless we become more like women. And it takes us one step closer to televised castrations, the ultimate reality show for American women.

Then there are those ridiculous TV commercials. One after another portrays the typical American male as a moron who cannot function without the constant "aid" (usually in the form of eye-rolling, laughing ridicule and rescuing) of a woman. Among the first of these ads was a classic Cheerios spot.

The scene opened at the breakfast table, where two kids were sitting with Dad while Mom prepared food at the kitchen counter. The dialogue went something like this:

Little girl: Daddy, why do we eat Cheerios?
Dad: Because they've got fiber and they're good for your heart.
Little girl: Did you ever eat stuff bad for your heart, Daddy?
Dad: …Sure, until I met your mom.
Mother: Daddy did many stupid things before he met me.

If you want a snapshot of how men have become weakened, this is a perfect example.

What Daddy should have replied to Mommy's putdown: "But the dumbest thing I did was to marry your disrespectful, patronizing mother."

What would you say if your wife tried to castrate you in front of your kids like that? Unfortunately, most men don't say anything. When a woman berates you for virtually everything you say and do, you tend to shut down. Men have been trained to keep their emotions inside and not "feel."

What the Cheerios TV commercial guy did was smile ruefully and finish his cereal. Then he probably went off to work to bang his secretary, who wasn't trying to cut his balls off on a daily basis. When their affair was discovered, people, especially women, rallied around the castrating wife and helped her take the poor guy to the cleaners. Today, he'd lose his house, his car, his savings, his dog, his big-screen TV and custody of his kids.

A recent Lysol commercial depicts a man racing around his home holding a cell phone to his ear while his wife reminds him of all the housework he is supposed to do in her absence. The implication is that she is off earning the bacon while he's home cooking it. She wears the pants while he wears an apron.

Sitcoms and TV commercials reflect what has happened to traditional roles in our society. But they also help shape and condition our thinking. We've seen such negative images so often that we've become inured to them.

We have allowed apathy to keep us from pushing for passage of the Equal Rights Amendment to the U.S. Constitution, despite the fact that it has gone to Congress every year since 1923. This amendment would, at last, level the playing field on which men and women co-exist. It would also prevent women from having *more and better* rights than men, especially in divorce cases.

What does the feminization of the American male have to do with divorce? Actually, it goes right to the heart of divorce, and it explains the shabby treatment we receive before, during and after a marital breakup. Women want us to submit to their every whim. They want all the rights for themselves and all the responsibilities for men.

It is no surprise that the changing roles of men and women in American society have helped drive up the divorce rate. Changing roles have meant changing expectations. While women have become socialized to expect too much, men have been socialized to expect too little. In the end, very few of us are getting what we want.

The simple fact is that we are all flawed, regardless of gender. Nobody can change anyone else. The only person you can change is yourself. And it's appalling that generations of American women have missed the boat on this one. If they really need to change someone, they should start with the faces they see in their mirrors every morning.

Instead of waiting for men to make things happen for them, women should practice their "equality" and start making things happen for themselves.

The male backlash has already begun.

Many American men are now looking for foreign women and dating and marrying across ethnic, cultural and racial boundaries. There are women in other parts of the world who still respect and appreciate maleness; women who don't think we are inherently flawed creatures in need of mothering. Most of these women are from other cultures where women are still happy letting men be men.

Change Your Dating Habits
to Improve Your Mating Habits

Many guys are fixated on certain physical types of women or physical attributes in women. Many guys, for example, have a "thing" for blondes with big chests.

If most of the women you've ever been with were blonde, consider changing your habits. If you have not had good luck with your old preference, maybe it's time to turn over a new leaf and graze in a different pasture.

You just might find yourself gawking unashamedly at dark-haired, dark-skinned Asian, Black and Hispanic women. The more foreign and exotic-looking the women, the better many men like them. After all, many foreign women still respect men as people. They are not hell-bent on changing us, beating us down or making us over in some women's magazine or *Queer Eye* notion of perfection.

Males still have strong tendencies to fixate on physical quali- ties such as hair color, body type, breasts, legs or buttocks while we overlook the more enduring qualities such as honesty, gen- erosity, integrity, respect and compassion. Which qualities would better serve a long-term relationship? And which quali- ties would better serve a one-night stand?

Maybe you are the kind of guy who has always been attracted to big-breasted, blue-eyed blondes with small waists and flat stomachs. You may have dated, gotten involved in rela- tionships with or married and divorced a number of women who fit that description.

But what happens when the physical qualities change and the whole basis of your attraction is gone? This is not meant to imply that certain physical types are either good or bad for long-term relationships. The point is that it's unwise to choose your long-term partners based exclusively on their physical appearance.

Go out on a limb, if you must, for that is where the fruit is.

If you're only attracted to one physical type, fine. Just don't marry them or have children with them unless they meet your core criteria. If you're looking for a real committed relationship, consider a woman who won't take you to the cleaners or put you through the kind of financial and emotional misery you'd become accustomed to when you were dating and mating busty blue-eyed blondes. Focus on the enduring qualities mentioned earlier.

When all else fails, there's nothing wrong with "singlehood."

The fastest-growing trend in America today is the single-person household. For the first time in our history, there are more solo households than there are traditional households made up of husbands, wives and children. In fact, more than 27% of American households now contain one person (58% of these are women, by the way). And that number has been rising steadily since the 1970s (along with the divorce rate). If you decide to remain a bachelor, embrace and celebrate the freedoms that go along with it. You're not alone.

The Ultimate Health Tips

"Wisdom consists of the anticipation of consequences."
– Norman Cousins, 1912-1990

Too often, we lose sight of ourselves after we have been through a divorce. We neglect our physical, intellectual, emotional and spiritual health.

This is a time when you need to take very good care of yourself. Get plenty of rest. Eat a balanced diet of vegetables, fruits, whole grains, fish, nuts and lean meats. Drink lots of distilled water because all the impurities and contaminants have been removed by the distilling process. Exercise in moderation.

What exactly is moderation? According to the majority of recent research, taking a brisk 30 to 60-minute walk three to five times each week is sufficient for maintaining fitness. Men should also do regular strength training with weights or resistance machines. We lose muscle mass as we age. Strength training replaces it. Alternate aerobic activities such as walking, hiking, biking, swimming, rowing or running with your strength training sessions to get the best results. And don't forget regular stretching to maintain flexibility.

Exercise is also believed to contribute to higher testosterone levels, which also decline as we age. Testosterone is the natural male hormone that ignites our sex drive.

According to a physician friend of mine, 30 minutes of *continuous* walking each day is all the exercise that a human body needs, as long as you eat right, drink plenty of water and get the sleep you need every night. You don't have to spend hours in a gym or compete in triathlons to gain all the benefits of exercise. If walking bores you, turn your walks into nature hikes.

When it comes to exercise, more is not necessarily better. Professional athletes routinely exercise several hours each day and tend to die much younger (60 is about average) as a result of the incredible stress they put on their bodies and the cumulative effects of their physical injuries.

Limit alcohol consumption, especially if you think your situation is "driving you to drink." The decision to drink or take drugs is still yours, regardless of your situation. Alcohol and drugs may numb you to your problems but won't help you solve them.

Instead, spend some time in nature. Watch the sun set. Do a little stargazing. Find a new hobby.

Visit supportive friends and family members. Take yourself to the movies or a favorite restaurant. Read a good book. Go to a museum. Buy yourself something you've always wanted, if you can afford it after being taken to the cleaners. Take a chance on yourself.

Whatever you do, it's got to be about you now. You're not part of a couple anymore. You're taking care of number one. The sooner you accept that, the sooner you'll be able to move forward and get beyond the pain of your divorce.

If you haven't seen a doctor in a while, now is a good time for that complete "annual" physical you've put off for years.

Divorce is stressful for everyone. How we deal with stress can make a huge difference in our health.

Be sure to talk to your doctor about your split and how you are coping with it. Are you sleeping well? Are you sleeping enough? Overeating? Undereating? Abusing alcohol or drugs? Working yourself to death?

Many men cope with the stress of divorce by working harder and drinking more.

Resist the temptation to take prescription medications such as Prozac, Paxil or Zoloft to "take the edge off" or reduce the anxiety you feel. There are natural herbal remedies – St. John's Wort and Kava-Kava, for example – that will help you achieve virtually the same results. Do some research before you take anything to determine what side effects these remedies may cause. And remember that exercise is the most effective stress-buster of them all, as long as you do it in moderation. Exercise is also a natural mood-enhancer because it raises serotonin levels in the brain. Along with exercise, make sure you eat right.

What constitutes eating right? Today, there is so much junk food and processed food available, and so much bad diet and nutrition advice floating around, it's hard to decipher the truth from the trickery. After reading and listening to all the "advice," I've come to the conclusion that it's easier to remember which foods are good for you. The list of evil foods that wreak havoc on your body is virtually endless.

Instead of wasting your time and money on 100 different fad diet books, find a Post-It® note or an index card and jot down the following – your new food-shopping list:

Vegetables
Fruits
Fish
Lean meats (beef, pork, veal)
Poultry (chicken, turkey)
Whole grains
Nuts
Beans

It's that simple. Those eight items, along with distilled water and nonfat milk, should comprise your permanent daily diet.

Everything else – pizza, pastries, pasta, bread, potatoes, cheeseburgers, hot wings, frozen dinners, doughnuts, french fries etc. – is pretty much garbage that provides nothing of value for your body or your general health. They're okay to eat on occasion but will never be the basis of a healthy diet.

Over 65% of American adults are now either overweight or clinically obese. It's because we've been following that ridiculous government food pyramid and assorted fad diets for decades, and we're getting fatter and fatter as a result.

Losing weight is simple, too. By eating the right kinds of foods in the right amounts and getting regular exercise, your body will eventually reach a healthy weight. There's no other secret formula or a magic pill that works while you sleep, no matter what those late night infomercials may tell you.

Avoid herbal and chemical appetite-suppressants or weight-loss pills now on the market. They are all based on unfounded claims and poor, if any, research.

One new diet aid claims to contain an appetite-suppressing ingredient taken from African bushmen. Why would an African bushman need to suppress his appetite? If you read *National Geographic,* you never see a fat African bushman. In fact, when you look at their pictures, you may be overcome by a strong desire to send them pizza and doughnuts.

When you hear outlandish claims, stop and think about them. Never accept anything at face value, especially if it comes from a government "health" agency or a business trying to turn profits.

To help your mind and spirit, find activities that you enjoy and are relaxing to you. Take up yoga or Pilates or kayaking. Meditation can also help you cope with stress. Spend some extra time at your church, temple or synagogue and get in touch with your spirituality. Read a good book.

Perform random acts of kindness.

There's an organization called Soul Graffiti (www.soulgraffiti.com) that is devoted to performing and promoting random acts of kindness all over the world. At this writing, they have members in nearly 60 countries. They believe that, together, we can make the world a better place. While that may sound trite, it's anything but.

It's about karma. Karma comes from the Buddhist belief that the sum of one's actions in previous states of existence will determine the fate of one's future existences. When you create good karma in your life, you attract all kinds of goodness in return. Givers gain.

If you think of divorce as an opportunity for personal growth and a challenge, instead of as a personal failure or a setback, you will be well on your way to sound mental, spiritual and physical health.

Remarriage? Are You Crazy?

Men who remarry soon after divorce are either gluttons for punishment or they've become so feminized by previous wives that they cannot survive without them. If you need someone to cook for you and pick up after you and wash your laundry, eat out more, learn to cook or hire a maid. All these will cost you less in the long run than having a wife.

If you have already achieved most of your professional goals (if you haven't, you shouldn't be looking for a relationship), and you find a woman who isn't out to remove your body parts but wants to please you, then give your relationship time to develop before tying the knot again. Among Jewish people, this is known as the "four seasons" rule. Give your new relationship a full year to develop before you consider leaping back into permanency.

Most men believe in waiting about three years after divorce before they remarry. Many psychotherapists and marriage counselors agree. It takes most men about two years just to get over a divorce.

Once you get over a divorce, take some time for yourself. Consider what marriage is all about and decide whether you would be happier going it alone, playing the field or spending your life with one person "for better or for worse."

Marriage, in and of itself, is not a bad thing. In fact, in the best of marriages, it can be pretty close to heaven on earth. Your partner can be your best friend, companion, lover and someone to share every facet of your life with.

Consider that married men tend to live healthier and longer than single men and have sex about twice as often. Then, there's that undeniable sense of family and connectedness and belonging that virtually all human beings need, whether male or female — knowing that someone is always there for you who cares for you and loves you unconditionally.

Decades of divorce have eroded our sense of belonging. We've been pushed away and apart so often that we can easily lose sight of the value of family. As a society, we're quick to divorce, quick to sentence our parents to old-age homes and quick to turn against our children.

As men, we sacrifice everything to avoid pain. But, in so doing, we forget that pain is part of life. Ups and downs. Good and bad. For better or for worse. Those words mean something. Without pain, there is no pleasure. And without pain or pleasure, there is no life.

To remarry is to embrace life in its entirety.

What Do Women Want?

It has been said that the great Sigmund Freud's dying words, after counseling thousands of women throughout his professional life, were, "Women. What do they want?" If Freud couldn't figure women out, how are we supposed to?

The fact is, we don't know. And the reason we don't know what women want, and Freud didn't know what women want, is simple:

Women don't know what they want, just what they feel right now.

Picture women shopping, which is arguably their favorite pastime. Imagine that a new "Husband Superstore" has opened at a mall near you. This is a place where women can shop for new husbands from among many choices. It has five floors and the quality of the potential husbands rises with each floor. The only rule in this store is that once the woman chooses a floor, she must select a husband from that floor. If she does not select someone, she must leave the store, never to return.

Two girlfriends are shopping for husbands.

They stop outside the first floor where a sign says, "These men have jobs and love kids." One of the women says, "That's nice, but I wonder what's on the second floor."

At the second floor, the sign reads, " These men have high-paying jobs, love kids and are extremely handsome." The women think about it and smile, but they wonder what's on the third floor. So up they go.

The sign on the third floor says, "These men have high-paying jobs, love kids, are extremely good-looking and help with all the housework." Now, the women are licking their lips with anticipation.

"Very tempting," says one of the women, "but imagine what's on the fourth floor." So up they go to the fourth floor. The sign there reads, "These men have high-paying jobs, love kids, are great looking, help with the housework and are very romantic."

"My God," says one of the women, "but think what awaits us at the top."

The sign at the fifth floor reads, "This floor is empty and exists only to prove that women don't know what they want. Please exit the building and never return."

The Ultimate Personal Success

"There is only one success –
to be able to spend your life in your own way."
– Christopher Morley, 1890-1957

If ever there was a time for you to start living life the way you always wanted, it's now. As soon as I learned that my ex had remarried, I wrote a list of the things I'd always wanted to do and posted it on the refrigerator where I'd see it every day.

Near the top of my list, for example, was travel to Europe, which I did a few months after my ex remarried. I went to my first "rave" party four months after she moved out. It was everything raves are cracked up to be. Lots of nubile young women, lots of loud, pumping music, lots of dancing and lots of alcohol and drugs. I was easily the oldest male there, but it didn't matter and no one noticed my rapidly graying hair.

I attended a dozen concerts and two dozen parties in 12 months. I also dated dozens and dozens of women. They were all different ages and from all different ethnic, racial and religious backgrounds.

I stopped watching sitcoms and soap operas – daily fare when I was married. There are just too many more important ways to use your time than sit and watch other people doing things on TV. A reformed couch potato, I wrote a book and got it published.

Couch potatoes don't accomplish much in this world. They are usually idle dreamers who sit and wonder why other people have all the "luck." They don't understand that other people create their luck through effort and sacrifice. All those hours they piddle away watching TV can be better used actually doing something to better themselves.

True success is being able to live your life your own way, in your own style.

Once you find yourself alone, you have the freedom to do that. You have the freedom to come and go as you please. You have no one to answer to. You are free to pursue your goals and your dreams without guilt.

Your goal as a newly single man is to learn as much about yourself as possible. After being stuck in a marriage that was probably all about her, you probably don't know *you* anymore. Now is the time to get to know *you*.

Being single again, and wiser than you were five, ten or 20 years ago, is a blessing. It's a second chance for growth and rediscovery. It's a second chance to find yourself.

PART FOUR

Where You'll Find More Help With Divorce

"It's not what you have that counts; it's what you do with what you have."

– Unknown

The Ultimate Man's Resources

"Fortune favors the bold but abandons the timid."
– Latin Proverb

This section includes some helpful definitions of some of the divorce terms mentioned in this book and some others you should know. I have also included additional resources to help you obtain different kinds of help before, during and after your divorce. It is sad that there are so few resources strictly for men, but it is true. Yet, most of the resources I have listed are specifically for men.

Look on the bright side. At least you can take comfort in the fact that you don't have a million choices to make and you don't have to waste your time weeding through them all. The resources available are ample to help you achieve your goals. And that's what matters.

The Language of Divorce

Abandonment: If one of you leaves the marriage home without the other's consent, it may constitute grounds for divorce in some states.

Adultery: If one of you has sex with someone else, it may constitute grounds for divorce in some states.

Alimony: The "ransom" one of you pays to the other in exchange for freedom.

Child support: A sum paid by one spouse to the primary custodial spouse for the benefit of maintaining the children. Child support is non-tax-deductible.

Community property: Includes most of the stuff you acquire as a married couple, with certain exceptions, in some states.

Constructive abandonment: An odd legal term meaning the refusal of one spouse to engage in sex with the other (what's *constructive* about that?); grounds for divorce in some states.

Defendant: The person named in a divorce petition (also called the respondent).

Dissolution: What some states now call divorce.

Emancipation: The age at which a child is considered free from your responsibility; varies by state up to age 21; the moment when child support payments can stop.

Equitable distribution: What a judge considers a "fair division" of your assets, property and income.

Garnishment: When your employer pays your spouse directly and deducts the amount from your wages.

Grounds: The legal reason (e.g., adultery) for divorce; varies a great deal by state.

Joint custody: You share all responsibilities for raising your children even though you live apart; your children will divide their time with both parents.

Joint property: Also known as marital property, it includes property you acquire during the marriage; exceptions might include inheritances, disability awards and gifts received from a third party; varies by state.

Maintenance: The same as spousal support; an amount paid, usually by the higher-earning spouse to the lower earning spouse, to provide living expenses.

Plaintiff: The person filing for divorce (also referred to as the petitioner).

Postnuptial agreement: Also known as a separation agreement in which you and your spouse agree to present and future rights in case of a divorce or the death of a spouse; can be created at any time, with or without divorce.

Prenuptial agreement: A contract between two people who plan to marry and want to establish rights in the event of divorce or death of one spouse; if needed, you may not want to get married.

Process server: A person hired by an attorney or the court to hand-deliver the divorce summons to the "defendant" or "respondent" in the divorce.

Retainer: Payment made to secure the services of an attorney; like a down payment.

Retainer agreement: It's all about how much of your money the attorney gets until your divorce is final; highway robbery.

Separate property: Property acquired by a spouse before the marriage or after a divorce action has begun; the stuff you get to keep no matter what.

Sole custody: When one parent gets 100% custody of a child or children and can make decisions regarding the children without consulting the other parent; there are some exceptions according to various state laws.

Spousal support: Same as maintenance; an amount paid by one spouse to the other to help with living expenses.

Divorced Dads' Resources

National Fatherhood Initiative
101 Lake Forest Blvd., Ste. 360, Gaithersburg, MD 20877
Phone: 301-948-0599
Fax: 301-948-4325

The Fathers' Rights and Equality Exchange
701 Welch Road, Ste. 323, Palo Alto, CA 94304
Phone: 500-FOR-DADS
Web: http://www.dadsrights.org

The Single and Custodial Fathers' Network
Web: http://www.single-fathers.org

Single Dads' Resources

Parents Without Partners
401 North Michigan Avenue, Chicago, IL 60611
Phone: 800-637-7974
Web: http://www.parentswithoutpartners.org

Single-Parent Resource Center
51 East 28th Street, 2nd Floor, New York, NY 10016
Phone: 212-951-7030
Web: http://www.singleparentresources.com

Psychological Resources

Ackerman Institute for Family Therapy
149 East 78th Street, New York, NY 10021
Phone: 212-879-4900
Web: http://spacelab.net/ackerman/springwks99.htm

**International Association
for Marriage and Family Counselors**
5999 Stevenson Avenue, Alexandria, VA 22304
Phone: 800-545-AACD

Financial Resources

National Foundation for Consumer Credit
8611 2nd Avenue, Ste. 100, Silver Spring, MD 20910
Phone: 800-388-2227
Web: http://www.nfcc.org

Pension Rights Center
1140 19th Street NW, Washington, DC 20036
Phone: 202-296-3776

Information Resources

Recommended Books:

Good Men: A Practical Handbook for Divorced Dads, Jack Feuer, Avon Books, 1997

Fathers After Divorce, Terry Arendell, Sage Publications, 1995

Live-Away Dads: Staying a Part of Your Children's Lives When They Aren't a Part of Your Home, Jack Feuer, Avon Books, 1999

Divorced Dads: Shattering the Myths, Sanford L. Braver and Diane O'Connell, Tarcher/Putnam, 1998

If Men Have All the Power, Why Do Women Make All the Rules?, Jack Kammer, self-published, 2003, www.RulyMob.com

Divorce Rules for Men: A Man to Man Guide for Managing Your Split and Saving Thousands, Martin M. Shenkman, CPA, MBA, JD, and Michael J. Hamilton, John Wiley & Sons, 2000

The Father's Emergency Guide to Divorce-Custody Battle: A Tour through the Predatory World of Judges, Lawyers, Psychologists and Social Workers in the Subculture of Divorce, Robert Seidenberg, William Dawes and Lawrence Pekmezian, JES Books, 1997. This book is highly recommended for men going through divorce, with or without children. It's also a tremendously insightful resource for men, regardless of where you are in the divorce process.

Here's an excerpt from a review in *The Liberator*, a newsletter of the Men's Defense Association, in December of 1997:

"This is a startling book, and not altogether what one might expect. It is, as its title indicates, a self-help guide; but it is also a political manifesto that opens a window to a world of struggle most people are unaware even exists.

"Everyone has heard the story of a father devastated in divorce-custody litigation – losing his home and children, and driven to bankruptcy as a result of child support, alimony and legal fees. Until now, though, one might have thought these were isolated instances. In The Father's Emergency Guide to Divorce, fathers'-rights activist Robert Seidenberg, writing with the legal insights of divorce attorney William Dawes, starts with the assertion that an abusive legal culture is the norm and that the brutalization of fathers in family court is an everyday occurrence.

"From the outset, The Father's Emergency Guide to Divorce differentiates itself from other books on this subject by focusing not on the written law but on what actually happens in a divorce-custody conflict. It describes the typical patterns of behavior of the main actors in the drama – fathers, mothers, judges, lawyers, psychologists and social workers; and the typical patterns of events. Drawing on his own observations and those of attorney Dawes, and combining these with the results of formal studies, Seidenberg offers a series of disturbing revelations.

"The book is a curious mix of practical advice and political commentary. It works because fathers in custody battles have arrived at a turn in life where the personal and political coincide. This book is a valuable resource for men in divorce cases and lawyers; it is also a worthy contribution to discussion in the areas of judicial culture and gender studies."

Online Resources

The following websites will provide you a wealth of information about divorce, state laws, formulas used to determine child support and much more. If you think your marriage is headed for the toilet, do some research. Gather as much information as you possibly can, whether you are initiating the divorce or suspect her of initiating the divorce (the signs are there if you look for them). Do what most lawyers recommend to their female clients. Jump-start your divorce by doing your homework and prepare to negotiate with your soon-to-be ex from a position of strength.

Divorce Central, http://www.divorcecentral.com

Divorce Online, http://www.divorce-online.com

Men's Movement, http://www.vix.com/pub/men/orgs/orgs.html

Divorce Source, http://www.divorcesource.com

Divorce Magazine, http://www.divorcemag.com

Divorce Net, http://www.divorcenet.com

Smart Divorce, http://www.smartdivorce.com/support.htm

Divorce Wizards, http://www.divorcewizards.com/

FindLaw, http://www.findlaw.com

American Civil Liberties Union, http://www.aclu.org

World Wide Web Virtual Law Library,
http://www.law.indiana.edu/law/v-lib/lawindex.html

http://www.menforjustice.com

http://www.cafeshops.com/mensbiz

http://www.fatherhood.org/

http://www.glennsacks.com/

http://www.mensactivism.org/

For Fathers: www.menstuff.org/fatherstuff/current.html

For Parents of Kids & Teens: www.menstuff.org/kidstuff/current.html

For Men's Health: www.menstuff.org/healthstuff/current.html

For Men's Issues: www.menstuff.org/mensissues/current.html

For Relationships: www.menstuff.org/relationstuff/current.html

For Sexstuff: www.menstuff.org/letstalkaboutsex/current.html

For Nonprofit Men's Organizations: www.mencare.org

For Men At Risk: www.menatrisk.org

Epilogue

I hope you will use all the ideas and resources available in this book as you attempt to survive your divorce and establish your freedom. Get smart about your situation. Take positive action to protect yourself against a greedy and unscrupulous ex-wife or lawyer.

Don't become yet another sad, lonely, broken, financially strapped ex-husband who has all but lost the will to live. It doesn't have to be that way.

It can and should be much better. You *can* survive divorce with your health, sanity, sex life, spirit and finances intact. You *can,* if your situation warrants, lose your spouse and keep your house. You just have to set your mind to it. Make all other considerations secondary until you're not only living for yourself but living your life to the fullest.

You can look at divorce as a kind of death. Or you can look at it as a new lease on life.

I hope you have learned something of value from my personal experiences, too. I hope you save thousands of dollars on your divorce by following this book's advice, negotiating with your ex and avoiding attorneys and the court system.

And I hope you emerge from your divorce as happy, healthy and confident about your life and your future as I did. In the end, I lost my spouse, kept my house, regained my freedom and rediscovered myself. Now, with the help of this book, you can, too.

About the Author

Howard Brian Edgar was born in New York City's Harlem in 1950. He received his bachelor's degree in English and Fine Arts from Clemson University, Clemson, SC, where novelists Mark Steadman and H. Barry Hannah were his mentors.

He has earned his living almost exclusively as a writer since 1975, when he began as a copywriter with a Madison Avenue ad agency. Later, he wrote weekly opinion columns and covered health, politics, crime, medical and environmental issues as an investigative reporter and columnist for two Florida newspapers.

From there, he joined the corporate world as a senior writer and video producer for a medical rehabilitation and fitness equipment manufacturer. During this time, he wrote extensively about health and fitness-related issues for physicians and physical therapists, including Pat Croce, who owned the Philadelphia 76ers of the NBA and the Philadelphia Flyers of the NHL, and now appears regularly on TV as a sports personality.

More recently, Howard has been a sports writer, a creative director and a senior staff writer for the nation's leading medical practice marketing firm. He has won over 50 creative, inspirational and leadership awards, including *Writer's Digest* awards for screenwriting and short-story writing. He is also the co-author of *The Ultimate Man's Guide™ to Internet Dating*.

A combination of personal experience and journalistic curiosity led him to spend the last several years researching the American divorce phenomenon. He interviewed hundreds of men, women, divorce attorneys, psychologists and judges, monitored dozens of divorce cases, not to mention surviving 24 years of marriage and two divorces of his own in preparation for this book.

He also followed his own advice: He lost his spouse, kept his house and found a far better life with his health, sanity, spirit and finances intact.

He currently lives in Huntington Beach, California, with his wife and son.